Family business models

Family business models

Practical solutions for the family business

Alberto Gimeno
Associate Professor in Business Policy and Director of the Advanced Management Program (AMP), ESADE Business School, Spain

Gemma Baulenas
Family Business Knowledge S.L.

Joan Coma-Cros
Family Business Knowledge S.L.

palgrave
macmillan

First published 2010 by
PALGRAVE MACMILLAN

Palgrave Macmillan in the UK is an imprint of Macmillan Publishers Limited, registered in England, company number 785998, of Houndmills, Basingstoke, Hampshire RG21 6XS.

Palgrave Macmillan in the US is a division of St Martin's Press LLC, 175 Fifth Avenue, New York, NY 10010.

Palgrave Macmillan is the global academic imprint of the above companies and has companies and representatives throughout the world.

Palgrave® and Macmillan® are registered trademarks in the United States, the United Kingdom, Europe and other countries

ISBN 978-0-230-24652-2   hardback

This book is printed on paper suitable for recycling and made from fully managed and sustained forest sources. Logging, pulping and manufacturing processes are expected to conform to the environmental regulations of the country of origin.

A catalogue record for this book is available from the British Library.

A catalogue record for this book is available from the Library of Congress.

10   9   8   7   6   5   4   3   2   1
19   18   17   16   15   14   13   12   11   10

Printed and bound in Great Britain by
MPG Group, Bodmin and Kings Lynn

CONTENTS

Figures

Annex

FOREWORD

In the early 20th century, American sociologist W. I. Thomas won fame with the statement: 'If men define situations as real, they are real in their consequences.' This fundamental observation on human behavior, now known as the Thomas theorem, became a cornerstone of contemporary sociology. The idea that our perception of the world determines our mindsets, and that these in turn guide how we manage the surroundings of our lives and the architecture of the institutions we create, is not new. In fact, like all important ideas, it has a long history. Even Plato preached it with his metaphor of the cave, at the dawn of Western culture. Its 'constructionist' advocates in philosophy and psychology include figures of the stature of José Ortega y Gasset, John Dewey, Herbert Spencer and Sigmund Freud himself.

The ideas gathered together in this book emanate from this intellectual tradition and make an extraordinary contribution to both research on and the practice of the family business. Alberto Gimeno, Gemma Baulenas and Joan Coma-Cros derive their concepts from a thorough empirical investigation and show us once again that Kurt Lewin, the father of social psychology, was right when he stressed that 'There is nothing so practical as a good theory.'

On the basis of an analysis of more than 1,500 Spanish companies, the authors narrow the field down to six archetypes of family business (The Captain, The Emperor, The Family Team, The Professional Family, The Corporation, and The Family Investment Group). Each of these archetypes describes a structural configuration of the family firm at a different stage of development, with its corresponding parameters of complexity, efficacy and risk. The basic assumption is that what works like a dream in one type of family business may be a recipe for disaster in another. Furthermore, these six archetypes not only constitute a useful typology for segmenting the universe of family businesses, but also describe the mindsets that business leaders possess regarding their systems.

The use of complexity as a parameter integrating a wide range of family and business factors that determine the adaptability of the family firm is of great conceptual efficiency. Complexity offers a common denominator that allows comparisons within the broad universe of family businesses. It also acts as a bridge to connect this work to organisational paradigms that are already well established. According to the authors, the antidote to complexity is the development of the necessary structures to manage it. When structures are inadequate to respond effectively to the degree of family and business complexity, structural risk grows. Without a doubt, the model they propose has a conceptual elegance that is very appealing to those of us who do research on the family business. Like all useful models, it fulfills a heuristic function and raises new questions and therefore new lines of research, such as:

- What factors affect business leaders' attachment to their mindsets?
- What conditions are required in order to bring about a change in leaders' mindsets?
- What happens when the same business family includes leaders with implicit and contradictory mindsets on the future framework of the family firm?
- What conditions help or hinder structural change?
- What relationship exists between structural risk and the continuity of the family business?
- Where is the structural risk threshold that a system is capable of withstanding before it becomes endangered?

Moreover, this approach serves to remind us of the innate plasticity of the family business. Their ownership control gives business families a great deal of leeway regarding how to set up their management and corporate governance structures. In fact, this research supports the idea that family business leaders forge organizational architectures in the likeness of their own mindsets. They do so because they can do it without significant interference from external forces such as the regulations governing listed companies. The malleability of the family firm constitutes a competitive advantage that gives entrepreneurs the necessary flexibility to find creative organizational solutions to the particular problems of their respective families and businesses. However, this plasticity also poses a considerable risk, as the universe of feasible solutions with the circumstantial profile of each company and family is not infinite. Therefore, effective management depends on how skillfully leaders can manage structural risk, by anticipating the levels of complexity of their families and companies and intervening with the right structural solutions. This requires leaders with the necessary capacity for self-reflection to be able to identify the assumptions and prejudices arising from the dominant mindset at the time, and the necessary courage to change their mindset when circumstances so require. This is the only way to achieve the adaptability that is needed in order to attain continuity from generation to generation.

Practice shows us that business leaders find it difficult to recognize and set forth their mindset. Above all, they are averse to recognizing how their mindset modulates their ability to diagnose the circumstances of their companies and families correctly when they evolve towards new levels of complexity. This is what the renowned Harvard psychology professor and colleague of mine Daniel Gilbert calls 'presentism', i.e., the cognitive difficulties we human beings have in imagining what our personal, family and business circumstances will be like in the future. In fact, we are imprisoned by the present because it forms part of our mindset – there is a symbiosis between the circumstances we experience and the mindset we use to manage those circumstances. As a result, when the world changes we are slow to react appropriately. Leading the continuity of the business effectively requires breaking this symbiosis and getting away from the reference framework we use to interpret our present surroundings faithfully.

The model presented by Gimeno and his colleagues provides several useful tools to help business leaders to escape from the mental prison created by their mindsets. Firstly, the ideas gathered together in this book give us a panorama of future destinations taken by family businesses in order to drive the planning of continuity. By doing so, the authors stimulate leaders' imagination. The six structural archetypes are in fact a snapshot of a hitherto unfulfilled 'imagined possibility'; they bear a resemblance to the 'business dreams' I myself have described.

Secondly, the authors not only describe destinations but also explain the routes to follow in order to reach a particular destination in the future. Depending on where the entrepreneur stands at present, this focus will give him or her an idea of the challenges that will be encountered in the course of evolution towards another structural model, more consistent with the level of complexity that is expected with the change of generation. The authors forewarn business leaders and improve their ability to anticipate coming events.

Thirdly, this approach offers a language that encourages dialogue and the creation of a shared narrative in business families regarding what there is *today* and what there could be *tomorrow*. In other words, the model helps to forge what I have called a 'shared dream' focusing on the change process and facilitating collaboration between the owners. By introducing a logical framework, the business leader can identify with a particular archetype, and so feel that his or her mindset is 'normal', and even appropriate under certain circumstances. In turn, this recognition opens up the possibility of a reflection on the need for less reactive change, and gives hope of a more impartial analysis of the present and future situation of the system. It is no longer a matter of justifying oneself; the problem is not that the leader is no good any more; the problem is that his or her mindset – which was extremely useful to get us where we are today – has to adapt to the circumstances that lie ahead. The authors acknowledge that shedding a mindset is far from easy and will always provoke resistance. One of the advantages of this book is that it provides a practical framework enabling leaders to 'save face' when they set about managing a change process.

For more than 20 years now, Spain has pioneered the development of the family firm. The creation of institutions such as the Family Enterprise Institute (IEF), the development of the network of chairs on the subject in numerous universities, the advancement of research at prominent institutions such as ESADE, and the continuously growing awareness of family business leaders of the need to empower themselves on a lifelong basis, has created a climate that is conducive to excellence. This study is a fruit of those efforts. It only remains for me to celebrate this achievement with my colleagues, encourage them to carry on their work and thank them for this magnificent contribution to our field.

Ivan Lansberg, Ph.D.
Lansberg, Gersick and Associates
Kellogg School of Management

ACKNOWLEDGMENTS

This book is the fruit of the effort and collaboration of many people and institutions that with enormous generosity have contributed their knowledge, experience and support to make it possible. We have the ambivalent feeling of making what we hope to be an important contribution to the field of family business and at the same time having 'appropriated' the work of many others. But such is the creation of knowledge: a small contribution that attempts to add something to the much that has already been done by others.

This book can only be understood in the context of ESADE. An institution that stimulates creativity, rigor, and the contrasting of knowledge and opinions. At ESADE the invitation to rigorous innovation forms part of a culture in which knowledge and experience are shared and multiple opportunities are offered.

We owe thanks to many people at ESADE, and it will be impossible to name all of them. One person is the fundamental cause of the existence of this book: Professor Adolf Vilanova. A pioneer in Europe of the study of family business, he created a powerful approach to family business management, the Four Planes Approach. His excessively self-demanding attitude prevented him from publishing it, and as a result it was only accessible to those of us who have had the good fortune and the privilege of being his disciples and followers. This book is indebted to Adolf.

The part played by the Department of Business Policy, and especially its director for many years, Marcel Planellas, has been a determining factor. His high standards, support and encouragement have seen us through to the end. The discussion sessions with our colleagues in the departmental Research Seminar,* organized

*Although the list is long, we would like to take this opportunity to thank each of the members of the seminar for the contributions they made to the development of this book: Luisa Alemany, Ernesto Amorós, Eugènia Bieto, Agustí Canals, Xavier Gimbert, Tamyko Ysa, Laura Lamolla, Carlos Losada, Javier Nieto, Eusebi Nomen, Pedro Parada, Manel Peiró, Marcel Planellas, Diego Torres and Lourdes Urriolagoitia.

by Marcel, questioned and enriched the foundations on which this book is built. We would also like to thank Xavier Mendoza for his work as co-author of the scientific work on which this book is based. The support of Montse Ollé, director of the Department of Business Policy, and Eugènia Bieto, director of the Entrepreneurship Institute, has been constant. The assistance lent by Carlos Losada has also been definitive for persevering in this line of work. The support of Simon Dolan has been key for inciting the interest of the English editors in our work.

In addition to Adolf Vilanova, there are four more ESADE professors who have made a crucial impression on this book: Eduard Bonet, Jaume Filella, Marià Corbí and Willem Saris. All four are people whose humanity and humility come from having succeeded in transforming knowledge into wisdom. This book breathes the Constructionism we learnt from Bonet, the subtle understanding of leadership processes that we were taught by Filella, the importance of ideological constructions conveyed to us by Corbí and the power of quantitative analysis that we were shown by Saris.

Joan Sureda and Joan Manel Batista have also had a determining influence on this project. Both came running countless times to help us out of the blind alleys we kept wandering into. María José Parada has also been of inestimable help in refining and adjusting the concepts discussed in this book. And we thank Joaquín Uriach for his generosity in proposing his experience as a basis for discussion and debate.

Our friends at ORT in Uruguay are also strongly present in this book. We will never be sufficiently grateful for their invitation to propose a non-conventional approach to family business management in their programs. Here we must mention 'el gran Gastón', Gastón Labadie, with his ability to give meaning to the various partial results we obtained, long conversations with Marcel Mordezki, and the support given by Anahir Benelli for the use of our methodology right from the start.

Another aspect in which we will fall short, no matter how much we highlight it, is the support received from the Instituto de la Empresa Familiar (IEF), especially Fernando Casado and Jesús Casado. Fernando was making a commitment when he chose to support a group that was proposing a different way of looking at family business management, and his promotion of the FBK-Diagnostic tool, the basis of this book, was an act of trust. We are grateful to him for believing that we were capable of proposing an analytical approach to family business management.

We thank Jesús Casado for his on-going support in getting the family business self-testing project accepted by the Regional Associations of the IEF, to which end he accompanied us all over Spain.

The project, *Radiografía de la Empresa Familiar Española* (Spotlight on the Spanish Family Business), has represented a milestone in the development of the knowledge contained in this book. We thank the Regional Associations and their directors for their support, especially Vicenç Bosch, Marilena Jover, Eduardo Estévez, Antonio Hernández and Mario Carranza.

The project, which is central to the development of this book, was made possible by the support of BBVA. This institution not only provided considerable financial backing but also invited many of their clients to participate in the project, thus making it a success. Behind institutions there are always people, and BBVA would not have backed this project had it not been for the enthusiastic support of Pedro Fontana.

This book would never have seen the light of day if the three authors had not coincided in Family Business Knowledge (FBK), a family business consulting and advisory project that brought us together some years ago. The possibility of modeling existing knowledge in the field of family business and creating an expert system capable of proposing useful solutions was the vision that got us to this point. Ricardo Zamora, Anna Mitjans and Josep Closas were essential for making the leap from a conceptual model to an expert system, as was the work of Lita Guilló, the person who is always behind everything we do. This book is also the fruit of her excellent work.

Our clients have been an extraordinary source of learning. Each case in which we have been involved has served us to improve and to gain greater insight into the situations family firms have to face. They have been of key importance for our understanding of the complex phenomena that we are now attempting to help to grasp and manage.

The support of the international community interested in family business has also been of great importance. The congresses and meetings of the Family Firm Institute (FFI), Family Business Network (FBN), IFERA, EIASM and FERC have for years enabled us to discuss our thoughts with colleagues and business families, thus notably enriching our work.

Obviously, we have incorporated the entirety of the knowledge that has been generated on family business. Within this extremely wide spectrum, we pay special tribute to the thought of Ivan Lansberg and Peter Davis. They framed a vision of family business of which we consider ourselves to be followers. In particular, Ivan dared us to make proposals that were far removed from dominant doctrine, giving our morale a huge boost.

A number of 'giants' of science and thought have generously offered us their 'shoulders' to stand on, through their works. Among others, we are especially indebted to thinkers such as Bateson, Gell-Mann, Herbert Simon, Kuhn, Lakoff, Ludewig, Luhman, Minuchin, Ortega y Gasset, Prigogine, Wagensberg and Watzlawick.

We wish to express our gratitude to our Spanish editor, Joan Amat, whose reflections helped us to make major changes in the book. Also the Palgrave Macmillan-team, Stephen Rutt, Eleanor Davey-Carrington and Shirley Tan, for supporting this endeavour and making possible the publication of this book. Also the translator of the English version, Toby Willet, who did an excellent job.

Lastly we would like to thank our respective partners, Marcela, Carlos and Marysún, and Lorenzo, Claudia, Victoria and Helena for their enormous encouragement and patience.

Many thanks to everyone.

What does this book offer those interested in the family business?

This is a book about how to manage the family business, and our intention is to help the reader build better managed and more stable family firms. For this reason, we consider that it is recommended reading for all those with an interest in the family business: members of business families, members of senior management in family firms, consultants, scholars of the phenomenon, and indeed anyone simply interested in the subject.

This book is the fruit of 20 years' work in this field. We have studied the literature on the subject, and we have been in contact with specialists and business families all over the world.

Our aim has always been the same: to gain a better understanding of the workings of the family business and to generate approaches allowing the best possible management of the family/business relationship. We have pursued a twofold goal: the business family should be satisfied with the relationship, and company results should likewise be satisfactory. As we have justified in our previous works, these two goals reinforce each other.

When business families understand the nature of the tasks they need to undertake, they act accordingly – and in most cases effectively. The important thing for the family is to be aware, and to make the right diagnosis of their situation as a family business.

This book is based on the enormous amount of data we have gathered using the FBK-Diagnostic expert system. This has given us the opportunity to work with detailed information on more than 1,200 Spanish family firms, thus allowing us to contrast our points of view and forcing us to rethink our approach in order to make it consistent.

The reader will see that this book is organized differently from any other book on the family business he or she may have read before. It seeks to create a map enabling the reader to know when and why it is important to apply each of the aspects of family business management that have been developed over the last 30 years. Our interest is focused on offering a road map for senior managers and business-owning families in order to help them define where they stand, where they want to go and how.

In Chapter 1 we present the history of family business management since it was first identified as a specific aspect of management. We briefly present the contribution made, in our opinion, by each different tendency, together with its possible limitations.

In Chapter 2 we introduce the family business management formula. The purpose of this formula is to show that family businesses differ. We hold that the complexity profile of the family business is a useful and practical way of grasping these differences and defining what kind of management to practise.

In this chapter we propose a way to define the structure of the family/ business relationship, which comprises a variety of inter-related aspects, both hard and soft.

In Chapter 3 we introduce the idea of family business models, that is, the idea that family businesses can be grouped according to type. We describe the set of characteristics of each of these models.

In Chapter 4 we address the consequences for management that derive from the various models. The reader will see how each model has its own challenges, and why so many well-intentioned undertakings end in failure.

In the annex at the end of the book we present a detailed account of those aspects that we consider should be managed in the family firm. We recommend those families wishing to further develop their family/business relationship structures to use it as a reference document and guide.

We hope that this book will be useful to the reader, and that it will help to strengthen the fabric of family businesses, which are the foundations of the world's economies. The family business is the best form of business organization when it is capable of bringing together aspirations and combining efforts, when it is capable of enriching the achievement of one in the continuity of the achievement of many, and when it is capable of respecting its past by transforming it into its future.

History of family business management

In this first chapter we will discuss the main milestones in the brief history of family business management, in an attempt to provide the reader with a better understanding of the approach we adopt and the contribution we wish to make through this book.

The history of business management dates back to the 19th century. In the Western world, the industrial revolution was the origin and cause of great transformations. The confluence of machinery and socio-political changes were to bring about the birth of a new type of economic organization: the modern business enterprise.

Javier Nieto[1] gives an excellent account of the evolution of management science, focusing initially on organization of labor and production (Henri Fayol) and developing towards people management (Frederick Herzberg), administration (Herbert Simon), the creation of structures (Alfred Chandler) and the elaboration of strategies (Kenneth Andrews).

Although an important current of management innovation and conceptualization was developed in Germany,[2] it was in the United States that management science really took off. The first business school in the world[3] was founded there in 1881 thanks to a donation by the industrialist and philanthropist Joseph Wharton.[4]

Ownership of many large American groups gradually dispersed, as the mechanism most commonly used to fund expansion was the stock exchange. Logically, the most innovative companies were those that developed most, and it was they that attracted most attention from management science.

Ease of access to information about listed companies was also a factor here. Researchers tended to study flagship companies and those to which they had easy access. It is also true that leading corporations in this field have been those most inclined to promote studies analyzing their own managerial practices.

Thus, it was the major listed corporations of the United States who staked out the playing field of management science, through motivation management (IBM), the creation of organizational structures (General Motors), corporate strategy (General Electric), commercial distribution (Sears), marketing (Procter & Gamble) and financial management (JP Morgan).

Companies were studied depending basically on their size. A whole set of theories were developed for the management of large corporations, while the only references to family businesses were as special cases of underdevelopment.

The relationship between a company and its ownership was only analyzed in the specific case of listed corporations, where relations between shareholders and managers were strictly established. All other companies were regarded as 'non-listed', the 'other businesses', and no more attention was paid to them. They were less developed enterprises that were supposed to evolve naturally in the direction of listed corporations.

It was not until 1976 that two Harvard professors, Louis Barnes and Simon Hershon, published a paper in the *Harvard Business Review* in which they propounded that family firms did not constitute an underdeveloped stage of listed corporations, but were a stable form of competitive organization in their own right. Even at this early stage, Barnes and Hershon identified succession as the chief problem for these companies.

Thus, for these authors:[5]

> According to recent research, family businesses evolve into publicly-held companies less often than we think. Given this constancy of lineage, the only thing that can be done to forestall those grim episodes connected with succession to the throne 'that damage the organization as well as the family' is recognition by the patriarch that both he and the business must

change. For the company to grow it is essential to remove the reins from the old man's hands. When management moves from one generation to the next, the transition is often far from orderly. In addition, as the company develops, there is a need for a management style that goes beyond survival thinking, and entrepreneurs tend not to be reorganizers.

Some years later, again in the United States, family business began to have its first experts: Leon Danco, with his program of seminars for family entrepreneurs and the publication of the first two books on family business,[6] and Peter Davis, who in 1980 set up the first academic program in family business at Wharton. His first paper[7] was the first study to present a truly in-depth analysis of issues specifically affecting family firms, yet today it is still very relevant and a worthwhile read for anyone interested in gaining a better understanding of this field.

In the past 30 years the discipline has evolved a great deal, both conceptually and with regard to its application. At present we can identify five main approaches to family business management. Each has its own focus on different management aspects and practices. Each stage has made new contributions to the previous ones, improving on its shortcomings.

Evolution of perspectives
Issues facing family businesses
Succession planning
The family constitution
Family business governance
Family communication

Figure 1.1   Management perspectives of family businesses

First perspective: issues facing family business

This was the initial stage of the 'discovery' of family business. Experts became aware of the existence of a multitude of family firms and their associated problems.

In his seminal paper, Peter Davis took a systemic approach to family business: the business and the family comprise two different systems that, by overlapping, transmit disorder to each other.

Figure 1.2 The family system and the business system

In this first stage, the experts identified the situations that occur in family business, focusing on the origin of confusion in the relationships that the family system introduces into the business system. Thus, they described problems at the time of succession, family conflicts, nepotism, interference from in-laws, and so on.

This situation is none other than the inevitable disorder that arises when two different systems come into contact.[8] The interpenetration of the two systems is reflected in the figure below.

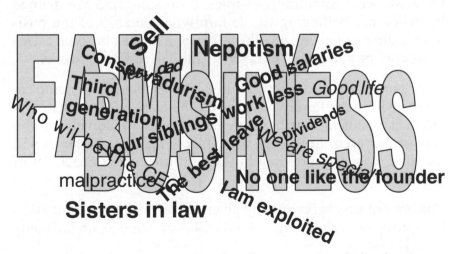

Figure 1.3 Disorder in the family system and the business system

In those early years, Harvard professor Renato Tagiuri published in collaboration with a young academic, John Davis,[9] an internal research document for Harvard University[10] studying the ambivalence generated within family business due to the interpenetration of family and firm.

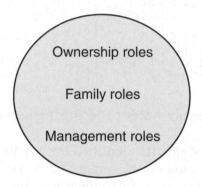

Ownership roles

Family roles

Management roles

Figure 1.4   Roles overlapping in family firms

These authors identified various different interest groups in the family firm, due to the roles that coexisted within it, and also the existence of simultaneous roles. A person's role was defined by his or her belonging to the family, ownership of the business and/or management. This arrangement has become extraordinarily popular and is known as the Three-Circle Model.

This approach has been very useful for understanding the problem generated for the family business by the clash of interests of its different members, together with the existence of individuals who play two or even three roles, with the confusion this creates and the difficulty of responding in the right measure to each set of interests.

This model was subsequently given an evolutionary dimension by a group of authors led by Kevin Gersick[11] and again including John Davis.

These authors proposed an evolutionary timeline in these three dimensions. This model makes an important contribution in that it highlights the existence of differences between family businesses;

a family business will differ depending on the stage in which it finds itself with respect to each of the three dimensions.

Gersick, Davis, Hampton and Lansberg defined in 1997 family business according to three dimensions or axis: business axis, family axis and ownership axis. According to these authors, family business evolves through different phases in each axis:

Business Axis phases

- Start-up
- Expansion-formalization
- Maturity

Family Axis phases

- Young business family
- Entering the business
- Working together
- Passing the baton

Ownership Axis phases

- Controlling owner
- Sibling partnership
- Cousin consortium

The problem with this model is that the ownership axis and the family axis refer to the same reality. The ownership axis refers to family relationships (founder, siblings, cousins), while the family axis refers to the details of the life cycle of the founding generation, and is therefore an extension of one part of the ownership axis.[12]

The contributions of this stage are important in that they define many of the situations that occur in the family firm, and provide an understanding of the problems that arise in those situations. These approaches are meaningful insofar as they have made it possible to start looking for solutions to the problems.

Second perspective: succession planning

Barnes and Hershon's 1976 paper, mentioned above, initiated the field of family business, paying special attention to succession as the main hurdle family firms have to overcome.

Succession has been identified as the great problem for the continuity of family firms. One of the most recurring facts in conferences on family businesses is that 70% of them succumb in the transition from the first to the second generation, and only 15% reach the third.

This figure, which is usually interpreted in a misleading fashion, is based on a study conducted by John Ward in Illinois on a sample of family businesses in the manufacturing sector, in which the frequency of businesses is observed by generations.[13]

Since its publication, this figure has been repeated over and over again as if it could be extrapolated to the entire world population, and above all, the way it is presented at conferences on the subject tends to assume causality. That is, it is assumed that the fact of being a family firm predisposes a business to fall by the wayside in 70% of cases in the transition from the first to the second generation, and that half of the survivors do so in the transition from the second to the third for the same reason.

This is a mistaken conclusion, as studies conducted on non-family businesses show relatively similar business mortality rates, and so a cause-effect relationship between a hypothetical disappearance of 70% of family businesses and the problems involved in succession is difficult to uphold.

This is not to say that succession is not a very important issue. Not only the experts but also all those with practical experience of a family firm know that at the moment of succession a whole series of problematic situations arise that could have been avoided. Such problems can be overcome through succession planning.

This perspective has proved to be very valid, and has helped a great many family businesses. Those managerial approaches that stress the importance of succession planning consider that it is a difficult process for the person who is going to be succeeded, especially if that person is the founder. The business is, in a way, the businessperson's life.

Managerial perspectives that focus on succession planning have been useful most of all in aspects related to ownership succession, and much less so with regard to management.

Basically, there are three main difficulties in considering succession as 'the big issue' for family business:

a. Succession is not a point in time but a very long process. The generation in power involves the next generation in the management of the firm 58%[14] of the time. In other words, more than half the time a given generation is in power it coincides professionally with the previous or following generation. As a result, managerial perspectives that are oriented towards planning for the 'changeover' have to a large extent been only partly successful.
b. Another aspect that has led to succession planning approaches being only relatively useful is that they have focused on 'model repetition',[15] i.e., the replacement of one executive with another, or several acting as if they were one. A successful succession in fact very seldom repeats the model; it usually entails a change of family business model.
c. The third difficulty has to do with long-term planning. The recommendations that have usually been made from this quarter require anticipating decisions that will affect the management of the company in the next generation. This means being 15 or 20 years ahead of the next generation's managerial needs, bearing in mind that the outcome of those decisions will be manifest 30 years on.

It is rather utopian to suppose that it is possible to foresee today who should manage the company 15 years from now, with a view to that person being at the helm for another 30 years.

The proposals of succession planning are very clear when analyzed ex post, that is, when a problem is analyzed and it is observed that there is a particular cause that should have been avoided. This approach ignores the difficulty of predicting that which has yet to happen, whereas it is easy to deduce the necessary prevention mechanisms once events have occurred.

Managing requires working ex ante, i.e., ahead of events, so it is necessary to take into account the almost unlimited number of situations that might arise. Given that this is impossible, we can say that succession planning is important but that the results are less useful than a retrospective analysis of past management might seem to suggest. Prescribing the past is easy.

Third perspective: drafting a family constitution

Family constitutions were also popular for some time, and to some extent still are. Managing a family business was associated with 'drafting a constitution'.

A family constitution is a system of rules for the family/business relationship. The logic behind this perspective is that although the rules of the game are laid down by the first generation in the first generation, in subsequent generations it is much more difficult to define a set of rules among all those involved in the 'relational game'.

By his or her own idiosyncrasy, it is the founder of a business who defines the rules. However, the question arises of who should define the rules in the following generations, when no single sibling or cousin has either the power or the legitimacy to do so on his or her own, as they are all on the same level. Several experts realized that this caused serious distortions in the family firm, and the managerial response was that the business family should come to an agreement on the rules defining their relationship with the business. In other words, they should draft a family constitution.

The family constitution is a system of rules governing the relationship between the family and the firm. The first family constitutions on record date back to the late 19th century and were drawn up by the great Japanese business families (Sumimoto, Mitsui).[16]

Spain is the country in which the family constitution has become most popular as a management tool. It has been used as a rule-making process dealing basically with the aspects of property (who has what ownership rights), money matters (who has rights over what income, whether in the form of salaries, dividends or any other company revenues), employment issues (conditions for working or being promoted in the company), succession in ownership and management, and the definition of mechanisms for entering or exiting the ownership group. Family constitutions usually also include a statement of the family's values.

The family constitutions that have been created fall into three main categories:[17]

- Ownership protocols, which focus primarily on the rights and obligations inherent in ownership, paying less attention to managerial aspects and very little to the issue of succession.
- Future protocols, which focus on introducing order into both ownership and the issue of succession. On the other hand, there is limited emphasis on management practices.
- Management protocols, which focus on aspects that favor the professionalization of management practices, paying very little attention to the rights and obligations inherent in ownership. The main purpose of this type of constitution is to limit access to the company by family members with the wrong profile.

Family constitutions have been a great help in the management of the family firm, and they have made two main contributions. First, they have highlighted the importance of the change from one generation to the next, and have been a useful tool for making this change.

And second, they trigger dialogue and conversation. In the course of drafting a family constitution, the family members talk about the issues that affect them as a business family. This often leads them to tackle subjects they have never addressed before.

Like the previous approaches, family constitutions are insufficient if taken as the firm's one and only management tool. In our opinion, this approach has four main disadvantages.

- The first and chief disadvantage is that families very seldom have a clear idea of how to go about redefining their rules. Many family constitutions comprise rules that are 'socially desirable' but are not necessarily those that the business family in question has actually proposed to incorporate or internalize. Frequently, constitutions are drawn up that have more to do with how the family would like to see itself a few years from now.
- The second drawback with leaning too heavily on this management tool is that it is often turned into a way of controlling the next generation; a way of getting the upcoming generation to abide by the rules. Logically, these rules are never put into

practice, with the sole exception of those required by the resulting legal framework.

- The third difficulty of the family constitution, understood as the firm's one and only management tool, is that is that it hems the family firm in. Often the most highly developed constitutions are those that seek to anticipate a huge amount of possible future situations, which forces them to go into a great level of detail. This very level of detail is what ultimately makes the family constitution a straitjacket.
- The family constitution has too often been used to prescribe rules for others, and too seldom for oneself. This tends to mean avoiding the issues that really need to be tackled, as these issues concern the present protagonists of the family business, and focusing instead on 'how the next generation should enter the business' or 'how many prestigious master's degrees they should have'.

Fourth perspective: governance

The governance perspective has basically revolved around the creation of various decision-making bodies or areas for the family business. Three main areas can be differentiated: the area of ownership, represented by the Family Council; the area of corporate governance, represented by the Board of Directors; and the area of management, represented by General Management and the Executive Committee.

The need for a Board of Directors was recognized very early on by family businesses, basically replicating in the family firm the model represented by listed corporations. John Ward, another of the great experts in the field of family business, stressed the importance of this body in his celebrated 1988 book *Keeping the Family Business Healthy*,[18] and a few years later he devoted a book specifically to this issue.[19]

Much less attention has been given to the Family Council. Although experts agree about its importance, it is not clear what part it should play. Even the most thorough books on the subject, for example Neubauer and Lank,[20] endow it with such vague responsibilities as 'governing the family' and 'performing a positive function in family/business relations'.

The main contribution of this approach is its dynamism. It abandons the idea of regulating and stiffening the system, opting instead to create different decision-making levels to deal with different issues.[21] With the introduction of these governance structures it is possible to make important changes in the family business, thus overcoming some of the chief difficulties of the perspectives mentioned above.

This approach does not require either detailed anticipation or exhaustive planning, as the idea is to create competent governance structures that are capable of making the right decisions at each moment.

The Family Council precludes one of the main drawbacks of the family constitution, namely that of the family tending to define rules that are desirable from a social point of view but that they are unlikely to put into practice. These governance structures make it possible to go ahead with agreements that the family has reached but is incapable of implementing.[22]

The approach taken by those experts who place special emphasis on governance structures has some significant disadvantages.

- Just because a body exists doesn't mean it works.
  Having a governance body (a Board of Directors, for example) is one thing; having one that works – that performs a governance function in the family firm – is another. There are a host of family businesses with a Board of Directors that hardly functions as such.[23]
- General Shareholders' Meeting.
  There is enormous confusion as to which responsibilities lie with the General Shareholders' Meeting and which with the Family Council, and as to whether one incorporates the responsibilities of the other. In practice, this means that these bodies are set up but it is unclear how the relationship between them should be structured, with the resulting loss of the contribution that they should make.

Fifth perspective: family communication

The development of communicative and relational aspects is another facet of family business management that has attracted the attention of many experts. The Family Firm Institute (FFI),[24] an international organization founded in Boston in 1988 and comprising the world's principal family business consultants, defines family relationships as one of the aspects to incorporate into family business management.

Communicative aspects have been added to the range of family business management resources on the basis of consultancy practices originating from the United States, with the incorporation of psychologists and especially family therapists into the field of family business.

For the professionals who defend this approach, the key factor for a family firm to work properly is that the relationships among its members must be open, clear and effective. To achieve this, relationships are nurtured through group dynamics that enable hopes, expectations and opinions to be shared.

This approach has also made a great contribution to family business management. The family dynamics most often organized by professionals that use this approach allow parents and their children, siblings and cousins, to spell out aspects that it is essential to be able to talk about.

Management perspective	Main advantages	Main disadvantages
Issues facing family businesses	Firms become aware of the nature of their problems	Describes situations but not management practices
Succession planning	Stresses the importance of dealing with succession	Difficulty of anticipating innumerable future possibilities
The family constitution	Defines rules in the family firm	Tendency to reflect 'wishes': how the family would like to see itself
Family business governance	Capacity to create a dynamic family firm	Little attention to the functioning of governance structures
Family communication	Provides a way to resolve conflicts	Confusion of communication as a means and communication as an end

Figure 1.5 Summary of family-business management perspectives

The limitation of this approach is that it is important to see communication as a means, not an end. This approach provides a useful tool, the development of communication, but it is not always capable of generating concrete proposals as to when the outcome of the family communication process is suitable and when it is not. The outcomes that result from applying this approach tend to favor the family and the family dynamics rather than the company and its interests, and therefore it may generate outcomes that are unsuitable despite being satisfactory for all concerned in the short run.

All the predominant approaches to family business management to date have made important contributions and propose valid management perspectives, whether they consist of the description of problems and situations, succession planning, the drafting of a family constitution, the creation of governance structures or the establishing of family communication dynamics. Yet they all have important shortcomings, for two main reasons.

They offer good responses to the management needs of family business, but they are partial responses. In the section above we have briefly outlined the strengths and the weaknesses of each different approach.

The second major shortcoming lies in our inability to know whether a family business is being correctly run or not. When has a succession been well planned? When is a family constitution suitable and when is it not? What is the most appropriate governance system?

In an attempt to integrate the entirety of the progress made in family business management, and at the same time to avoid the problems identified to date, the authors of this book embarked on a long research project that has culminated in a family business management formula and the identification of different types of family firm.

2

Family business management formula

In this second chapter of the book we explain some of the fundamental concepts of our proposal, which are integrated into a management formula. Through this formula the reader will understand why one family business is different from another, and how with time his or her own family business gradually changes.

The reader will grasp how to identify the structure of the family/business relationship in his or her particular case, and to assess to what extent that structure is appropriate. In this chapter and the annex at the end of the book we will present those management variables on which the family can take specific action.

Structural management of the family business

The basic idea of the Family Business Management Formula is to prepare the family firm to cope with the situations it may come up against. It attempts to approximate the type of situations that it is most likely to come across. This level of anticipation, unlike anticipation in detail, is easier to achieve.[1]

This avoids having to make detailed predictions of the solutions that all family businesses will have to seek in the medium to long run, which would be impossible, as the experience of the past 30 years of family business management has shown.[2]

It explains how as time passes both the family and the company become more complex, that is, that in both of them many more unexpected events will happen than are happening today, and that we cannot identify them a priori but they are going to happen, as a consequence of greater complexity.

Who can anticipate today that an unmarried niece will want to sell her shares because her future husband wants to set up a business? How can it be known beforehand that one of the shareholder brothers will fall out with the rest of the family because they won't let his son, who is now in primary school, work in the family business?

These events cannot be anticipated, but we can be assured that they are much more likely to happen in a complex family (for example, a second generation of four siblings coinciding with a third generation of nephews and nieces, some of them married and with children) than in a less complex one (a couple with two young children).

Accepting this way of viewing the family/business relationship means working with different ideas from those we are accustomed to. Clearly, the fact that there are no problems in an increasingly complex family today has absolutely no bearing on whether there will be tomorrow. Efforts should be focused not on preventing what is going to happen, which is impossible, but rather on establishing a type of family/business relationship that is capable of channelling and absorbing the events that are bound to occur.

The formula rests on an approach that is currently flourishing in all sciences, natural and social alike: complexity theory. We have borrowed three main concepts from this scientific approach: complexity, structure and stability (structural risk).[3]

Complexity

The reality of the family business is not dichotomous (with two possibilities, black or white, good or bad, appropriate or inappropriate) but fuzzy. In other words, there are degrees (or shades of grey). Our model presents all its variables from the perspective of greater or lesser development, as if we were evaluating them on a scale from 1 to 100.

Not all family businesses should be managed in the same way. Family business management should be different depending on the nature of the family firm in question.

Family businesses differ depending on their level of family complexity and their level of business complexity. Family and business complexity define the type of problems that the family business will face in the future.

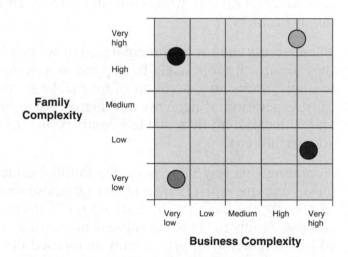

○ Fourth generation with 60 family members owning a multinational food company
● Group of cousins owning a property rental company
● Four siblings owning a chemical company with a global presence
○ Married couple running a restaurant

Source: Authors' compilation

Figure 2.1 Examples of complexity profiles

All four are examples of family businesses, but clearly the family/business relationship should be managed differently in each case.

Structure

The instruments for generating order in the family business can be divided into five main dimensions:

• Creation of institutions
• Differentiation of family and business

- Development of management practices
- Development of communication
- Preparation for succession

In turn, these dimensions are made up of a series of operational management variables, i.e., variables on which the business family can act directly in order to develop its structure. These variables appear in the figure below:

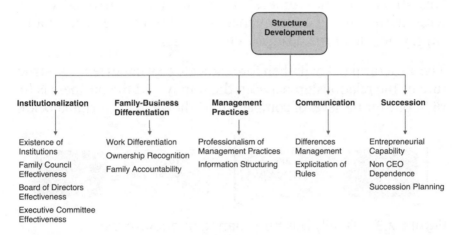

Figure 2.2   Dimensions of structure

Stability (Structural Risk)

Structure enables the family business to find the right solution to the situations it has to face. Therefore, the level of development of the family business (its structure) must be the right one for the level of family and business complexity.

A family business will have structural risk insofar as its structure is not sufficiently developed for its level of complexity. The greater the gap the greater the difficulty experienced by the family business in coping with the situations it is likely to face, and so the greater the risk.

The authors do not propose that family businesses should always have a highly developed and sophisticated structure to their family/ business relationship, but rather that this relationship should be gradually perfected as the family and the company become more complex. Thus, the companies in the example in Figure 2.1 should have different structures. The family and the business should be related differently in the restaurant owned by a married couple and in the multinational food company owned by 60 cousins.

The idea is not to apply costly solutions but to put into practice the right level to prevent the family business from falling into a situation of risk, i.e., an unexpected event destabilising it.

Destabilisation may unleash a chain of uncontrolled events with unknown end consequences (e.g., family break-up, bankruptcy or sale of the business, etc.).

The structural risk will therefore indicate to what extent the structure of the relationship between the family and the business is the right one for the level of complexity, as shown in the formula below.

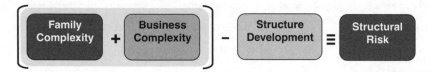

Figure 2.3   Family business management formula

The aim is to minimise the structural risk of the family business. Structural risk is the propensity for an unforeseen incident to unleash a sequence of connected events that are difficult to control. Thus, a quarrel between two brothers, the only partners in the firm, over a non-decisive decision such as the appointment of a member of the family to the post of production manager may degenerate into an ongoing feud and eventually lead to the sale of the company to a foreign multinational.

As the formula shows, the family business needs to reduce its structural risk. This can be done in any one of three different ways:

• By decreasing family complexity
  One of the brothers in the example above buys the other brother's 50% share in the company. Family complexity will decrease, and there will be fewer incidents with one owner than with two partners. Note that the figures of primogeniture tradition pursued precisely that end: to reduce family complexity.

- By decreasing business complexity
  This can be achieved by, for example, selling the business in order to create an investment company and then dividing this among several family members.[4]
- By developing a relationship structure between the family and the business
  This consists of introducing elements to channel and order the disorder that the family brings to the business. For example, a Board of Directors is created to include non-family members, and a General Manager is appointed from outside the family.

So, in accordance with our Family Business Management Formula, we believe that the relationship between the family and the business should be actively managed, just as sales or production are, and the goal of this management is to reduce structural risk. This can prevent unexpected incidents – which are bound to happen – from unleashing a series of uncontrollable events leading to unknown consequences.

Family complexity

Going back to the formula stated above, let us concentrate on its first component: family complexity:

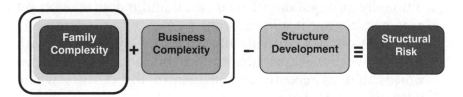

Figure 2.4   Family business management formula: family complexity

Historical evolution of the family business

Many family businesses began as small industries or shops. Activity was organized around the extended family, formed by the patriarch, his wife, the children, their spouses, siblings, grandchildren, etc. The maintenance of this group was guaranteed by shared work, with the resulting economic interdependence of its members and the frequent contact between them:[5]

> In earlier times two distinct types of activity were combined in family businesses and farms. A merchant might live with his wife and children in the back room of his shop, as bakers still do today in small French villages. Wealthier merchants might live in an apartment above the shop. [...]
>
> Lack of differentiation in space led to lack of differentiation in time. If customers found the doors of the shop closed, they did not hesitate to knock on the window of the back room where the family was eating, and someone would hasten to help them. Things began to change when the lady of the house, disturbed by a customer after closing time, ceased to accept the interruption as a matter of course and instead blurted out, 'We'll never have any peace around here, that's for sure!' At that point living in one's place of business came to be seen as a kind of imprisonment in work. People began to insist on privacy, and, in order to protect that privacy from invasion by customers, it became necessary to find living quarters away from the place of business [...].
>
> [...] The trend toward separate living quarters is unmistakable, as can be seen from a glance at the professions. Doctors, lawyers, and those quintessentially French professionals the *notaire* (notary) and the *huissier* (bailiff) are traditionally quite jealous of their status and independence, yet even here change is quite evident. [...]
>
> [...]Today the very private life is defined by contrast with working with working life. A clear boundary divides two worlds that as recently as the turn of the century where intermingled. [...]
>
> [...]A symmetrica evolution resulted in the reorganization of the workplace, from which all nonproductive functions were eliminated. [...]

The economic independence of each family group and the acquisition of a private home was one of the elements that brought about the transformation of the family model: the extended family was subdivided into multiple nuclear families.

This social evolution has further modified the family by incorporating a gradual separation between places and times for working life and private life. As a result, social complexity increases and family complexity decreases, the family being formed by a basic nucleus of parents and children.

In contrast, the business family still maintains bonds that are characteristic of the extended family, as we continue to find the circumstances for this to happen: economic dependence on the company founder or leader and frequent contact between its members. When it is the founder or some other family member who controls the business and determines the income of the rest of the family, the result is a situation of dependence that duplicates the patriarchal model. Equally, the existence of the business creates a series of bonds and a relationship between the family members that are lacking in other families, because they work together and see each other periodically. In fact, second or third cousins in a third, fourth or fifth generation business family keep up a frequency of contact that would be hard to find in a non-business family.

Family complexity is a consequence of the internal dynamic created when the family expands and the interrelationships between its members multiply, as do the number of events that might occur. The complexity of the business family is transmitted to the firm in its relationship of interdependence.

Family composition

The line defining who belongs to the family and to what degree is a blurred one. Although we have different names to determine kinship expressing closer or more distant ties (parents, children, grandparents, uncles and aunts, cousins-in-law, nephews and nieces, etc.), this is not the determining factor for defining the degree of belonging to the family group.

When a child draws his family he might put the dog almost in pride of place with its name underneath, and he might leave out one of his brothers or forget his father, or he might forget to put himself in the drawing. Does that mean that for that child the dog is a member of the family? It probably does, although he also knows that he, his father and his brother also belong to the family.

This spontaneous family composition is not restricted to children. Adults too might say: 'such-and-such isn't family; he's my wife's brother,' an indication of the fuzziness of the limits of who belongs to the family. Whereas this person considers that his brother-in-law does not belong to his family, someone else would say that he does.

Family composition has an objective side and a subjective one. There is a formal composition, defined by the structure of kinship, and a more personal and arbitrary one depending on the emotional bond: the perception of closeness or distance, of shared experiences, of feelings of affection linked to the relationships among the various family members.

Thus, the formal nature of the family composition can be depicted in a genogram. The genogram makes it possible to view the family tree over four or five generations with its respective ramifications. It also provides a graphical representation of the different levels of family: nuclear and extended.

(Gender differences are shown with a circle for women and a square for men)

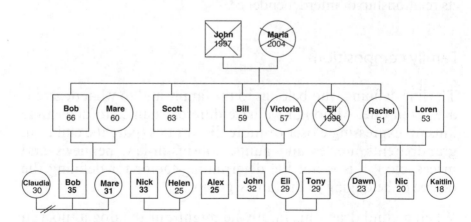

Figure 2.5 Genogram

A genogram like the one above can be used to reflect the life history of a family.

Family life cycle

All families have a time marked by the biological dependence of its components. Birth, maturity and old age are the natural way of things. Hence the various stages of a family are described in terms of a generational life cycle.

Functions of the family

The family fulfils two main functions: nourishment and socialization.[6] The former consists in protecting and caring for the physical and emotional development of the members of the family, whereas the latter is about conveying values, rules and social status to those members. In Western cultures, these functions are assigned mainly to the nuclear family, with greater or lesser participation from the extended family depending on the type of society.

Family identity

Cultural and social differences define different ways of organizing families in the performance of their functions: more or less differentiation between the nuclear family and the extended family; differences in functions depending on gender; a wider or a narrower gap between the private world and the public world. People, groups and societies have a host of different ways of doing things. But family identity, that is, the commitment to shelter the fragile and progressive growth of the human being within a family group, is similar in all cultures and periods.

The family provides its members with identity, security and equality:

• Identity. In the family, people represent an end in themselves. One has a right to belong to the family for the mere fact of having been born in it or accepted into it through adoption or pair bonding.

  Permanence as a member of a family is stable. Each person is a member of his or her family and will always remain so. He or she belongs to the family regardless of distance or proximity. It is his or her historical reference.

Although the fact of belonging to the family is stable, the functions performed within it change, in a process that develops from dependence to self-reliance. Over the length of our lives, we take on the different roles that are played in the family: from dependence as a child to exercising responsibility as a parent; from the relationship among the group of siblings, sharing a family, to the self-reliance of each of them along his or her own life histories.

- Security. The predominant relationships within the family are of an emotional nature. The members of a family are intensely involved with each other. Irrevocable bonds built on the basis of love and protection create a complex web of emotions, feelings and reactions in the family that is difficult to analyze objectively within the domain of rationality.

In the family, value lies in forming part of it. Each family member has value in his or her own right; his or her personal identity is complete. The important thing is not the particular capabilities or merits of each person, but the fact that he or she belongs. Each member has the right to belong by birth.

- Equality.[7] The distribution of resources is based on equality. The family share what they have on the basis of criteria of equality or need. Equality between its various members is claimed from a very early age. This criterion is modified by support for the weakest or the one in most need. Thus, for example, brothers and sisters want to be treated as equals, and if the parents buy one of them a motorbike when he or she turns the age of 18, the rest will feel that they are entitled to be bought a motorbike when they reach that age.

Often the criterion of need also prevails. In the case of a child with some disability, the family accepts that he or she must be given more support than the rest, given his or her greater need.

Families are succeeded generation after generation, retaining their identity and the recognition by its members that they share the history of a common stock. The business family adds to this the business as an identity factor among its members.

Family structure

Structure describes the series of actions and relationships that can exist among the members of a group. Family structure is made up of culture, hierarchies, norms and rules, and roles. Thus, in any family, everyone knows what is habitually done, how it is done, what is said, what is left unsaid, what is allowed, what is not allowed, what is usual, what is exceptional, who does what, who holds authority over what matters, what is right and what is wrong, and so on for a multitude of attitudes and actions.

Family structures are dynamic and evolve over time. A family with young children does not have the same structure as a couple whose children have grown up and now have their own families. In the former, the basic functions are care and attention to the children, whereas in the latter the family function leans more towards periodic reunions, shared celebrations, availability to substitute the parents occasionally to look after the grandchildren, etc. Similarly, the loss of a member or the incorporation of a new one will bring about changes in the group as a whole.

Any internal structure also establishes hierarchies, distribution of power, decision-making and internal control of its functioning, this process again being one of evolution in the development of any family. The limits, the norms and the demands that parents make of their young children and teenagers change when they finish their studies and enter adult life.

Furthermore, in the internal structure of any family there is a common culture, built through beliefs, values, experiences and past events. Family culture in all its breadth and diversity is passed on from generation to generation and has multiple expressions in its members' way of thinking, the expression of their emotions and their behaviour.

One of the expressions of family culture is through the norms and rules internalized by its members. Norms are related to the concept of what is 'right' inside and outside the family group. They vary with the evolution of the family, and it is therefore interesting to observe the flexibility of the family to adapt its norms to the situation required at each stage of the family life cycle.

The norms, i.e., what each family judges to be right, can be explicit or implicit. Explicit norms are those that are stated and repeated, and known by all its members, and failure to comply with them generates consequences that are likewise known by its members. 'In this household dinner is at nine o'clock' and 'the children have to tidy their own bedrooms' are examples of explicit norms. Generally the number of explicit norms in a family is quite limited.

Most norms in the family are implicit. They are agreements that govern the family's relationships and ways of doing things, but about which it is not usual to talk clearly. Fits of temper and decision-making processes are good examples of the existence of such norms.

Implicit norms exist in many areas. One example could be fits of temper, outbursts of anger, accusations and reproaches, and the reasons for them: can these emotions be expressed? In what way is their expression accepted? Is it acceptable to shout, or to run off to one's bedroom and slam the door? Can everybody do it, or only some, or no one? What is regarded as an insult in this family? Endless behavioural details stake out well-defined limits between what is tolerated and what is not tolerated in each particular family.

Decision-making is another example of the abundance of implicit norms. There are some families in which decision-making is governed by explicit norms such as where to spend the weekend or what sort of birthday parties to have, while in other families decision-making lies within the territory of parental authority and no negotiation is possible, again within explicit rules. Other families leave this compartment within the realm of the implicit, and it is never clear who will end up making the decision.

Family norms constitute a multitude of behaviours that are internalized by each family member. However, this knowledge of the usual way of doing things in his or her home is of no use for interacting with other families, even ones with similar characteristics.

Families progressively set up internal structures intended to provide them with order and stability. Although these structures have similar functions in all families, they are specific to each of them in that they reflect their particular vision of the world, their values and their way of fitting into the world.

The dynamic nature of the family structure enables it to adapt to the changes and transformations that occur in its social environment and at the same time maintain its stability and identity.

Indicators of the complexity of the business family

Family complexity and business complexity are two of the three components we use to determine whether the business is running the risk of destabilization.

First of all, we need to determine the variables that operate in the definition of greater or lesser complexity in a family. A family's relationship with the firm will be more or less complex depending on:

Number of members
Differences in life cycle stages
Number of branches or families
Different roles
Different life histories
Different interests

Figure 2.6   Indicators of family complexity

Number of people who make up the family
A family with ten members is more complex than one with five.

TIME

Figure 2.7   Increase in family complexity

A larger group of people means a larger number of differences, of diverse relationships, of resources of a varied nature. Therefore, the greater the number of members in a business family the greater the level of complexity, i.e., the greater the probability of many more different things happening.

In a family with 20 members there will be more internal differences: differences of age, interests, life situations, etc. It is likely that there will be groups with affinities (age, tastes, interests) and more than likely that there will be the occasional disagreement between some of its members or between groups of them. In order to maintain family cohesion and integrate major differences, it is important to have a wide range of resources for reaching agreements.

Different life cycle stages

Family complexity is affected by the different periods in which people find themselves. A person's level of complexity increases as he or she advances in the life cycle. In this way, a young man at the beginning of his career will add less complexity than when he is married and with children. Then he will have pressing financial and time commitments that will make him more demanding with regard to the business.

When his children reach working age, complexity will increase again, with the raising of the possibility of their working in the firm. The retirement stage will also bring complexity, as aspects will arise concerning inheritance, the meaning of what has been done so far, and the desire to go further.

The existence of family members passing through different stages of their life cycle will increase complexity. The fact of some family members having children aged five and others having children aged 25, for example, will make for different needs, but also greater difficulty in understanding others, given that reality is seen partially: differently at different times.

Number of family branches or families involved

A business family comprising parents and their children will have a different degree of complexity from one comprising a group of second cousins from different family branches, even though their origins can be traced back to a common stock. It is very likely that each family branch will have its own characteristics, based on the particular experience of each nuclear family.

Complexity increases when different family branches are involved, as each family or branch of the family group will owe loyalty first to its own branch and only secondly to the family as a whole. Each branch will tend to defend its own interests before the general interest.

In the case of a firm with more than one family this effect will be accentuated. Each member's loyalty to his own family will be far above his loyalty to the common project. If, in addition to this, branches appear in each family, the complexity will multiply.

Different roles (in the business and in the family) played simultaneously

Complexity increases as the number of family roles increases. When the roles are those of parents and children there is less complexity than when the roles extend to uncles and aunts, nephews and nieces, cousins, second cousins and so on. The bond that exists between siblings is different from that between cousins or second cousins, and so the complexity will be greater with five cousins than it will be with five brothers and sisters.

A wide range of roles can be played simultaneously, as a person might be a father, brother, husband, uncle, cousin and more, all at the same time. His relationship through each role with each family member will be different.

Different life histories

Family complexity will also be affected by its members' life histories. Each person follows a particular life path that gradually forms his or her being, thoughts and actions. The sum of the life histories existing in the family will be a factor contributing to determine its level of complexity.

As individuals, we interpret what we are confronted with in reality on the basis of our life histories up until that moment. The greater the differences between the life histories of the family members the greater the complexity, as the reality of the family business will be interpreted in more diverse ways.

If family members have different educations (e.g., in management and medicine) or different careers (e.g., a manager, a pianist and a teacher) or grew up in different countries or continents, complexity will grow accordingly.

One's life history is linked to one's personal and professional development: the sum of one's friends, interests and experiences. To give an example based on stereotypes, in the case of three siblings, the first conservative and traditional, the second anti-system and the third metrosexual and narcissistic, complexity will be greater than if these differences did not exist.

Different interests

Here we are referring to differences in interests regarding the relationship between the firm and each family member (economic benefit, prestige, job security, power, personal fulfilment, future rights, etc.).

The breadth of the family group results in a wide range of different interests among different family members. Diverse interests increase the internal complexity of the family group and call for the explicit management of these differences.

The interests of the various family members regarding the family business fall within any one of three main orientations:[8] protective, venture-driven and financial.

Protective orientation

This orientation seeks to maximise the contribution to situations of direct and basic family need, such as the income required for maintaining a family, together with non-monetary rewards derived from work (social status, self-esteem, occupying one's time, and so on).

A person with this orientation values the business for its capacity to generate employment and income for the family. The business should be at the service of the interests of the family. This profile is common among small business owners. They are unlikely to develop large companies, as their prime concern is to maintain a stable situation that suits their own needs and those of their family. For people with this approach, the business is 'obliged' to accommodate them by offering professional development and the ability to maintain a decent living standard for their family.

Venture orientation

This is the orientation of the person interested in developing and leading the business project. It is the dominant orientation in entrepreneurs who are committed to their venture. The aim is value creation through growth and expansion.

Sustained profit generation is seen as a necessity for the realization of the venture rather than a goal in itself. To this end, the business family is willing to sacrifice both part of its private consumption and alternative investments. The big family businesses have developed within this orientation, but there are also many small businesses that, although they have yet to achieve the growth they desire, exhibit a venture orientation.

For people in whom this orientation is dominant, the business is a platform for developing their dream and their vision. Interest lies not only in the business developing the venture envisaged by this person, but also in the fact of this person being the business leader in order to be able to put the venture into practice. 'This business is "my project" and I want to develop it "my way".'

The chief motivation is to run the business, and by doing so to channel its cash flows towards growth. Getting a return on the investment is not an important motivation.

Financial orientation

For people with this predominant orientation, the interest of the family business lies in the fact that it forms part of their assets, and should therefore be optimised in terms of profitability, liquidity, risk and so on. To this end, it is important for the business to be well managed. This person is not interested in running the business, but rather in the financial performance resulting from it being well run.

Ultimately, for a person with this orientation, the main interest of the family business lies in it yielding better returns than other alternative investments.

Mixtures of dominant orientations

By identifying orientations we are able to understand part of the diversity of interests that occur in the family business.

Orientation	Interest
Protective	Job and salary
Venture	Power and project
Financial	Profitability

Figure 2.8   Dominant orientations

Dominant orientations form radial categories,[9] i.e., there can be pure degrees and degrees that belong only partly or in combination. Thus, we frequently find mixed cases of protective and venture orientation ('I want to carry out my business project and I want to protect my children by having them work with me') or a combination of venture and financial orientation ('I want my project to go ahead but I want it to yield returns that are comparable to the alternative investments I could make').[10]

There is no reason to suppose that any of these orientations is better than any other, although they do have different consequences. The orientation depends on the values to which the person attaches most priority.

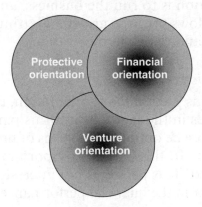

Figure 2.9   Dominant orientations as radial categories

The interests of the family as a whole can imply different complexity depending on the type of business family concerned. If all the members of the family have a protective orientation, the dynamic between them will focus on who works in the business and who does not, how much each family member earns, and whether there is room in the business for all of them.

If all the family members adopt a venture orientation, the focus will be on who is in charge, the nature of the project at hand, and who is at the helm. A person with a venture orientation will not be adverse to other family members working in the business, as long as he remains in charge.

When all the family members have a financial orientation, the centre of attention will be assets, i.e., who is entitled to what share, whether or not profits are sufficient, and to what extent there is a sufficient dividend or sufficient share liquidity to be able to leave the group.

When some family members operate with a protective orientation and others with a venture orientation, complexity will revolve around investment and risk. Those with a venture orientation will want to invest in new projects, while those with a protective orientation will ask themselves why they should complicate life and risk losing what they have attained.

When family members with a venture orientation coincide with others who have a financial orientation, the crux of the matter will be whether the family firm generates sufficient returns, whether there is too much risk concentrated in the family business, whether it would be better to invest in other projects, whether it is better to invest together or divide out the shares so that each can invest to his or her liking, and to what extent it is advisable to reinvest less and pay out more dividends.

The different dominant orientations at work should be identified in order to understand the complexity of the family firm.

Business complexity

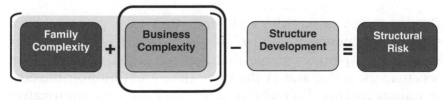

Figure 2.10   Family business management formula: business complexity

The concept of complexity is also applied to the business. A company will be more complex if it contains more elements and relationships within it, and if these elements are more closely related to more elements outside it.

The history of business is one of increasing complexity. Low-complexity preindustrial craft workshops gave way to factories built around large steam engines. The complexity of these factories rose again notably when the electric motor opened up the possibility of decentralized operations with several motors in one factory driving different machines at different speeds.

Complexity also rose with improvements in communication, both in the sphere of information and in that of the transport of people and goods. Markets went from being local to increasingly global, and this brought an increase in relations, with more and more diverse customers, more markets, more suppliers and more competitors.

The change from demand markets to supply markets also added to the complexity of businesses. The important thing was no longer just to produce. When productive capacity outstripped purchasing capacity, it was necessary to produce better and more cheaply. Then a time came when this was not enough and it also became necessary, as well as manufacturing and selling, to develop technology, design, innovate and provide additional services.

In recent years, businesses have been subjected to new demands to increase their complexity. The advent of scientific and technological production, computerization, telecommunications, the opening of markets and the emergence of new economic powers have created the need for increasingly complex businesses with the capacity to give a broader response to the environment in which they move.

Businesses are affected by changes that take place in their sector, and increasingly also by those that happen in other sectors. Companies emerge that achieve global leadership in less than 20 years, and at the same time great monolithic corporations collapse.[11] Global access is no longer the prerogative of the very large; today small local companies can also have global access.

Value chains break up. Many 'manufacturers' no longer manu-
facture anything, bitter competitors collaborate with each
other, intangible aspects come to dominate value capture, and
young people barely out of their teens create multi-millionaire
companies.

The financial economy takes on increasing importance as a
result of expectations generated by states of opinion based on
intuitions and feelings rather than hard data.

Value migrates ever faster between countries, companies and
regions. A country can be presented to the world as an exemplary
model for economic development and soon after just the opposite,[12] a company can be held up as examples of excellence[13] and
then suddenly disappear, and the same can be applied to entrepreneurs.[14] In short, we are witnessing the increase of business
complexity.

Independently of the general trend towards complexity, there
are notable differences between the levels of complexity of some
family businesses and others. Complexity will define the margin of
discretion and demands to which the family will be subjected.

Indicators of business complexity transition

The complexity of a business can be approached from several
different perspectives:

- Size. This idea probably requires little explanation. A company
  with 1,000 employees is more complex than one with 20. The
  systems of coordination, remuneration, promotion and training
  will have to be different, as will their exposure to internal and
  external upheaval. If we use turnover instead of number of
  employees as our indicator, the reasoning will be the same.
- Number of workplaces. A company with several workplaces
  is more complex than one with a single workplace, e.g., an
  assembly plant. More situations of a varied nature will arise
  in the former due to the physical distance between activities.
- Level of product diversification. It is also clear that the larger
  the range of products or technologies handled by the company

the greater the number of situations in which it will be
immersed. The complexity of a specialized company (Piaggio)
is lower than that of a diversified one (Honda).

- Level of internationalization. A highly internationalized company is more complex than one which only operates locally.
There will be more situations caused by the diversity of cultures,
languages, legislations, currencies, time zones, etc.

- Level of value chain integration. A company that performs
several activities in the value chain, such as obtaining raw
materials, manufacturing, designing and distributing (Zara[15]),
is more complex than one which focuses on few activities
(Nike). There will be more situations of a diverse nature due
to the need to coordinate activities, agents' interests, competitors at different levels of the chain, qualities, priorities, etc.

  Tenet Healthcare Corporation (a hospital chain) is more
complex than one which performs routine and repetitive tasks
(Quality Oil Company, a chain of gas stations). Doctors have a
higher level of independence and control over their own work
than a worker in a closely defined process such as serving petrol.

- The type of sector in which the company operates also entails
greater or lesser complexity. A company that is active in a sector
strongly affected technological change (Telefónica) is more
complex than one which operates in the food distribution sector
(Carrefour).

Size
Number of workplaces
Level of diversification
Level of internationalization
Value chain integration
Level of knowledge
Type of sector

Figure 2.11   Indicators of business complexity

Effects of complexity on the family business

The combination of family complexity and business complexity
forms the complexity profile of the family business. This profile
can be approximated using the variables that we have defined in

the above points. The complexity profile of the Spanish family businesses included in the FBK Database (2007)[16] is shown in Figure 2.12.

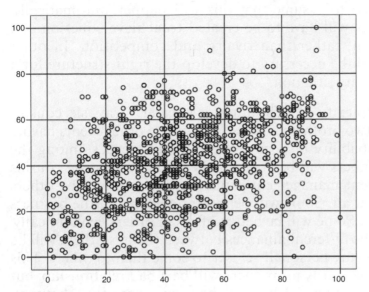

Source: FBK Database, Spain 2007

Figure 2.12   Complexity profile

This enables us to understand that family businesses are different depending on the complexity profile, as we discussed earlier. We cannot predict what is going to happen in each of those companies, but we can anticipate what sort of situation they will probably have to face.

As we have already mentioned, in a family firm with a more complex family we know that there will be more differences among its members regarding their skill profiles, needs, life histories, values as nuclear families, etc. Greater family complexity will mean bigger differences between them. As a result, a more complex family may introduce more disorder into the business.

So, for example, if a family wants the senior management of their company to be occupied by family members, but there are only two brothers of an eligible age for these posts, the issue will arise of how they should be coordinated in order to run the business successfully. And there will be the matter of how to ensure that the two brothers' cohesion is not diminished but actually reinforced by their professional relationship.

It is reckless to assume that this will happen automatically. Mechanisms will have to be created to achieve cohesion and coordination, rather than rivalry and competition. In other words, it will be necessary to develop the right structure for a low-complexity situation.

If the complexity of this family is greater – say, six cousins instead of two brothers – we can anticipate other events having a high probability of occurrence. The differences among the family members will be greater. There might be some cousins with excellent management skills, and there might be others with none at all. Some will be more interested in the business than others. Some will be better-off than others economically. There will be different alliances between them, so there will be cousins who are personally closer to some than to others. This does not necessarily mean there will be a bad relationship, but there will be more 'chemistry' between some than between others.

If they all want to be in management posts, the firm will probably start to have problems, as it will be extremely difficult to coordinate six senior managers who hold their posts because they are members of the family. This means they will have to decide who is going to work in the business and who is not, which is likely to cause arguments among them. Issues will be raised such as who should work and who should not, the size of the CEO's salary, what will happen to those who don't work, etc. The reader will have no difficulty in continuing the list of issues this family will probably have to tackle.

If, however, we are talking about 20 second cousins, other issues of a different kind will arise, in addition to the above. It is likely that each cousin will feel the need to defend his or her own branch of the family. The economic differences between them will probably be greater. The matter of how many dividends should be paid out will impose itself, and no doubt some groups will be more inclined towards large dividends, while others will be keener to reinvest.

Differences in dominant orientations will make their presence clearly felt. There might be some people who think the firm is badly run, and that the managers should be replaced. The managers may perceive these opinions as aggressions from discontented members of the family. Some family members might be interested in selling their shares. In short, the issues of ownership and demands placed on management will gain in importance.

All these issues derived from increasing family complexity generate dynamics that absorb the family's energy and undermine its cohesion. These dynamics have a negative effect on both the satisfaction of the family and the economic performance of the business.

This negative effect is not inevitable, and can be avoided through structure development. However, it will indeed be negative unless the family builds an appropriate structure for family/business relations, capable of channelling complexity and limiting the disorder that a complex family can convey to the business.

Structure[17]

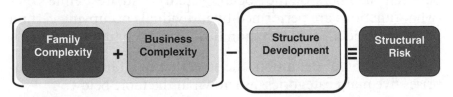

Figure 2.13   Family business management formula: structure development

A system is defined as a set of interrelated elements that are differentiated from its surroundings, even though it may have relationships of mutual dependence with these surroundings. This concept has been used widely in the study of the behaviour of groups of individuals, referred to as social systems.

All social systems are living entities, and as such are dynamic, with a wide spectrum of possible behaviors. Nevertheless, they reach high levels of order and certainty with regard to the behavior of their members.

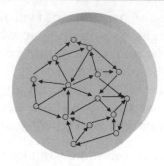

Figure 2.14 Representation of a system

This relative stability is due to the capacity for self-organization of living beings. The spontaneous emergence of ordered structures in open systems is widely established in nature.

In our approach we take the definition of structure as the internal capacity for self-organization of a social system. Within structure we include the notion of contexts (behaviors make sense according to the place and the situation in which they occur), we incorporate rules (explicit or implicit definitions of what can, cannot and should not be done in each place and situation), we create positions (hierarchies in the relationship between members of the social system), and we define roles (what functions are performed by individuals occupying certain positions) and also information flows and exchanges.

According to our definition, the structure of a family firm comprises five main categories, as shown in the table below:

Institutionalization	To what extent decisions are formed by different contexts or bodies.
Family/business differentiation	To what extent those who work in the firm are treated as professionals, and the shareholders as owners.
Management practices	How the company is run.
Communication	How personal relationships are managed.
Succession	To what extent the firm will be viable in the future without the present senior management.

Figure 2.15 Categories of structure in the family firm

Each of these qualitatively different categories incorporates a series of management dimensions. The categories themselves (for example, Communication or Succession) cannot be managed directly, but the management dimensions they encompass can be managed, as we will see in the sections below.

Institutionalization

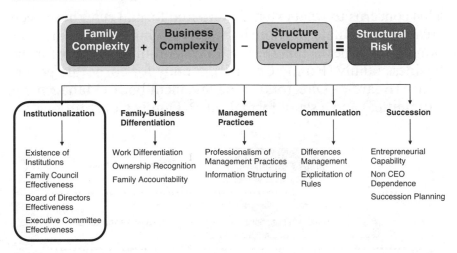

Figure 2.16 Dimensions of structure management: institutionalization

When the firm and family group grow beyond a certain size, a direct relationship between the two systems (family and business) becomes insufficient. In order to regulate the relationship it will be necessary to create properly differentiated spaces for decision-making and to establish rules for action.

This category includes the existence or otherwise of the following decision-making bodies and rules, together with the assessment of their functioning, if they exist:

- Family Council
- Board of Directors
- Management Committee
- Family Constitution

The institutionalization of governance in the family firm involves the development of four management dimensions, that is, four areas that can be managed and can therefore be modified.

- Existence of institutions
- Family Council Effectiveness

- Board of Directors Effectiveness
- Executive Committee Effectiveness

Existence of institutions[18]

This concerns to what extent bodies and formal rules have been created to regulate relationships. Thus, a high level of institutionalization means that there is a decision-making body for the business family (Family Council), a body for corporate governance (Board of Directors), a management body (Management Committee) and a set of formal rules (Family Constitution).

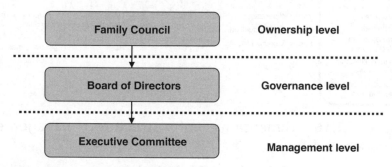

Figure 2.17   Institutionalization

Family Council Effectiveness[19]

We make a distinction between the institution itself and its functioning. The important thing for the system is not the existence of the institution but the performance of its function. Therefore, the Family Council Effectiveness will depend on the extent to which it fulfils its task.

The Family Council performs five main functions:

- To exert authority
  The assumption of authority by the Family Council entails:
  – Fixing the limits of that authority.
  – Appointing the governance bodies and deciding who will be in them.
  – Establishing criteria to determine who should take what responsibility in the company and what pay they should receive.
  – Determining the income of the owning family (dividends).

- Negotiating a 'management mandate' with the Board of Directors.
- Resolving unforeseen situations.
• To socialize
  To socialize a person into a system is to make that person party to the values, culture, behavior patterns and processes inherent in that system. To socialize the family means conveying, among other things, values, risk-taking ability, training and information, and behavior patterns leading to the responsible exercise of authority.
• To represent and transmit status
  Belonging to the Family Council is another way of 'belonging' in the family business. It is the task of the Family Council to represent the family as an institution in the social framework in which it moves.
• To encourage cohesion and develop an entrepreneurial spirit
  Family cohesion in a family business should occur through the construction of a common project that is capable of appealing to the willingness of the individuals involved. This cohesion should be built around shared information and the idea of entrepreneurship and creation.
• To fix limits and rules
  The Family Council also performs the function of setting the limits of family intervention in the affairs of the business. One common way of setting these limits in family councils is through the creation of family constitutions.

Board of Directors effectiveness[20]
The main function of the Board of Directors is to govern the company in accordance with the mandate previously negotiated with the Family Council. However, its specific functions are:

• To lend support to senior management
  This refers to support for strategic decision-making, regarding the technical quality of the decisions, their relevance over time and their acceptance by the organization.
• To monitor senior management
  This means controlling senior management in order to ensure that the executive power of the company is supervised and accountable. It involves aspects such as strategic decision-

making, evaluation of the performance of the management team, financial control, remuneration, auditing, etc.

- To develop, maintain and control distinctive resources and capabilities
  This means stimulating their development or capture, their use, application and protection, and preventing these resources from being transferred to or duplicated by other companies.
- To guarantee succession
  By this we mean creating management practices that develop the capabilities of the management team independently of those of the top executive, so that he or she can leave the post as harmoniously as possible when the time comes.
- To impose restrictions on the family
  This involves preventing the family from intervening in the business as a family (that is, with a family logic and criteria), by ensuring that the formal relationship with the managers is channelled through the Board of Directors.

Executive Committee effectiveness[21]

The company's Executive Committee is a collective management body. Depending on its characteristics, its executive scope will be greater or lesser. There are three types:

- Informative Executive Committee
  Members share information and the General Manager decides.
- Deliberative Executive Committee
  Members analyze and assess the information and subjects are debated jointly. If appropriate, the General Manager makes recommendations.
- Decision-making Executive Committee
  Senior management makes the highest decisions collectively within this type of Executive Committee.

The Executive Committee has direct effects on the functioning of the organization. It enables executives who have a centralized and intuitive approach to management to introduce more analytical elements into their decision-making processes. This makes it possible for the knowledge possessed by these executives to be stated explicitly, and for management talent to be nurtured with the organization.

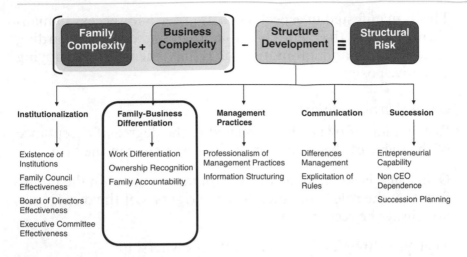

Figure 2.18   Dimensions of structure management: family/business differentiation

Family/Business differentiation

Family/business differentiation refers to the extent to which family members are capable of differentiating their rights, duties and behaviors depending on the role they are playing at any given moment. In other words, whether they are capable of clearly differentiating their rights and duties and how they should act when they find themselves in different contexts. Differentiating the family from the business involves the development of three management dimensions, that is, three areas that can be managed and can therefore be modified:

- Work differentiation
- Ownership recognition
- Family accountability

Work differentiation[22]

Work differentiation refers to the extent to which those family members who are actively involved in the management of the business are so because they belong to the family or because of their professional ability. The greater the presence of family criteria in decisions affecting the working life of the family in the business, the poorer the differentiation will be.

This is manifested in aspects such as criteria for access to management posts, the hierarchies that exist, and criteria regarding remuneration and promotion of family members occupying executive posts.

Ownership recognition[23]

Recognition of ownership is related to the degree of acceptance of the rights of the owners as the highest power in the firm.

Ownership is so often identified with management in the family firm that the role – and therefore the rights – of the owner may not always be recognized.

There are three fundamental rights of ownership:

- The right to have information about the progress of the company (right to information)
- The right to be taken into account in important decisions that may affect the owners' property (right of decision)
- The right to have economic returns and a certain amount of liquidity of their property (economic rights)

The necessary alignment between ownership and management should be built by managing the commitment of the shareholders to the business project, not by denying them their rights.

Family accountability[24]

To talk of exigency is to talk of the extent to which the fact of a family member occupying a post in the company merely implies the exercise of power or also includes the exigency of a certain level of performance.

Founders are subject to exigency from outside the company (competitors, customers, etc.), but not internally from company hierarchies or owners. Nevertheless, they are highly self-demanding, and this brings them to develop their company beyond their own levels of comfort.

Here we are not concerned with whether a family member is capable of being more or less self-demanding; rather, we want to evaluate to what extent the organization itself is exigent with all those working in it, whether they are family members or not.

Family accountability is about the family's mandate to the functional hierarchy of the company and the institutional structure to be demanding with the family members in accordance with the position they occupy.

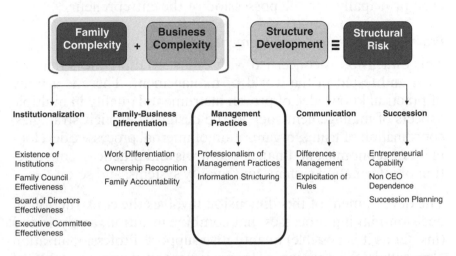

Figure 2.19 Dimensions of family business structure management: management practices

Management practices

The family firm tends to be dependent on the figure of the founder or some dominant family member. Such figures often run the firm in an 'unorthodox' way – which does not mean in the wrong way. The outcome may be extremely successful. The downside is that it is a sort of management that is highly dependent on the skill profile of one particular person, and when that person fails, so does the running of the business.

As the family business increases in complexity, its management should evolve in such a way as to take full advantage of the entrepreneur's vitality and drive, but at the same time to allow the business to be run according to criteria that are not accessible only to the entrepreneur.

This entails developing two main dimensions:

• Professionalization of management practices
• Information structuring

The first refers to management practices considered common in the basic aspects of management (we could call it an 'MBA style') and the second refers to the creation of systems and ways of working aimed at ensuring that knowledge is not only – or even principally – in the possession of the entrepreneur.

Professionalisation of management practices[25]

This dimension is concerned with managerial practices that are tried and tested in the world of management. There is a body of practical knowledge of proven instrumental quality in multiple aspects of management such as the design of explicit strategies, coordination of teams, organization of internal processes, development of economic and financial controls and practices, construction of information systems and quality systems, and so on.

The development of this dimension involves the construction of decision-making processes that combine intuition, analysis and (insofar as it is possible) quantitative support. Professionalization also entails the creation of management structures capable of making decisions that are decentralized yet in line with overall strategy, without this meaning loss of control by senior management.

Information structuring[26]

In this dimension we refer to both the quantity of information that an organization can encode (data) and the order and meaning it establishes within this data in order to be able to use it (information).

Structuring affects economical and financial information, management indicators, working protocols, definition of processes, patents, technical specifications, market surveys, performance assessment systems, etc.

Communication

Communication is an act that is derived from language and thought. We all think and speak, but we do not always find the right way to express what we mean to say, or notice when we are misunderstood. There are few sayings as equivocal as the one that goes 'People understand each other by talking to each

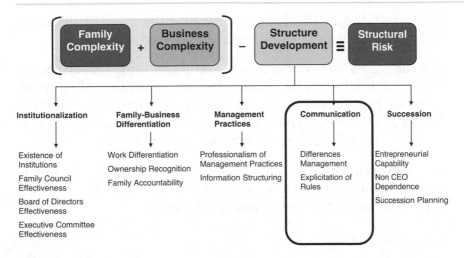

Figure 2.20 Dimensions of family business management: communication

other'; people may understand each other by talking, but they can also misunderstand each other.

Communication is good when it is possible to talk to everybody involved about everything. Everybody must be able to speak their mind without those listening feeling attacked or offended. This can be achieved to a greater extent by those who have developed communication skills and relational sensitivity.

A family that manages to maintain clear and fluent communication on issues linked to the family business creates a climate of trust among its members. Trust makes it possible to tackle disagreements openly, seek solutions together and reach agreements from a position of logic.

There are two management dimensions that need to be developed in order to improve communication:

- Differences management
- Explicitation of rules

Differences management[27]

Here we are concerned with how a family manages differences among its members in order to create cohesion around a project.

When we talk of differences we mean differences of interests, skill profiles, personal situations, roles played, etc.

Handling differences correctly involves recognizing that the members of the family can be 'equal' (they are all siblings, they are all linked to the business family, etc.) but at the same time 'different': they all have their own characteristics and their own nuclear family, and they can make different contributions and bonds.

Increasing family and business complexity will require the family to develop its difference-managing skills. Otherwise risk will grow, as in the other dimensions of structure.

Explicitation of rules[28]

All social behavior is governed by implicit or explicit rules, and therefore so is the family business. The rules of a social system are behavioral guidelines and limits for its members as a whole. The highway code may impose a speed limit of 120 kph, but that will only be a rule until such time as drivers take it on board as a behavior pattern.

The explicitation of rules is about a family's ability to state the behavioral rules existing between the family and the business in its family business system. This makes it possible to discuss the appropriateness of these rules, and if necessary to change them. The rules fixed (in the form of family constitutions) are often expressions of wishes, as the family is unable to accept the rules that are really governing their behavior.

Thus, the family must cultivate its ability to state the rules, as this is what will enable it to change them if they are inappropriate.

Succession

Succession in the family firm is related to the creation of conditions allowing the continuation of a successful business. The traditional approach of planning the replacement of the General Manager, although important, is clearly insufficient.

Businesses must display entrepreneurship, i.e., the ability to re-create the company around 'the new'. The next generation must therefore have the ability to build an entrepreneurial business.

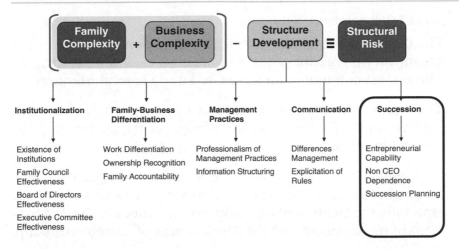

Figure 2.21 Dimensions of family business management: succession

Succession will also be possible insofar as there is low dependence on the top executive. The greater the dependence on this figure the more difficulties the next generation will have to carry on without him or her.

Entrepreneurial capability[29]

The development of companies requires vitality, the ability to undertake ventures. The creation of a business is the development of an entrepreneurial project. One generation's project is unlikely to be viable during the next generation. This is a mistake that has been made all too often in the family firm: to think that one generation can carry on the project of the previous generation by simply increasing the efficiency. In other words, doing the same, but better. This is why entrepreneurship is the foundation on which succession must rest.

Entrepreneurship can be manifested through the ability to generate a strategic renewal of the family group, but also through the ability to undertake new ventures within the group.

The company has to be capable of maintaining entrepreneurship, which does not necessarily mean that members of the next generation have to lead the projects. The whole enterprise has to behave as an entrepreneurial organization.

Non CEO dependence[30,31]

The top executive is taken to mean the person in charge of the organization, regardless of the name used to designate the post (those most commonly used are CEO and General Manager).

The top executive is a basic resource of many companies' competitive ability, for his or her knowledge, skills, relationships or leadership capacity.

Developing Non CEO dependence is closely linked to the whole range of dimensions of structure that we have dealt with above, especially the creation of an institutional structure, the development of management and the development of entrepreneurship.

The importance of this dimension does not lie in its manageability but in its accessibility; that is, business families should be able to evaluate to what extent their company depends on the top executive, and if this dependence is high, work towards reducing it.

Succession planning[32]

So far we have dealt with aspect relating to management succession, and now we will turn our attention to those relating to ownership succession.

Succession planning has a strategic dimension and also a legal and administrative one, mainly related with the transmission of ownership. From the strategic viewpoint, succession decisions have a direct impact on family complexity, and should therefore be tackled from that perspective. The legal and administrative component calls for several aspects to be taken into account: tax issues, wills, and agreements on property, corporate and economic matters.

3

Family business models

In this chapter we identify various types of family business, with the intention of enabling the reader to gain insight into his or her own family business by associating it with one particular type. We invite the reader to reflect on how his or her way of thinking affects the business and how he or she can drive it forwards in the future.

The profile of the family business studied in the work cited earlier[1] yields the following distribution (see Figure 3.1).

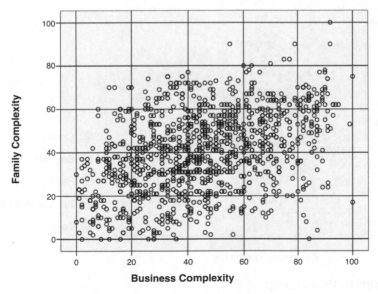

Source: FBK Database, Spain, 2007

Figure 3.1   Complexity profile of the Spanish family business

This graph, comprising 1,237 family firms, allows us to identify the differences among them. Uncertainty arises when we try to establish categories, in other words, when we look at these differences and decide that they are great enough for two different family firms to be allocated to different types.

If we feel intuitively that certain family firms are different, we should also ask ourselves what features (variables, a researcher would say) make them different.

Using the data in the FBK Database, we were able to identify five main categories of family firms, on the basis of their level of complexity and their degree of structure development. This statistical treatment[2] enables us to clearly identify the following family business models:

- Captain Model
- Emperor Model

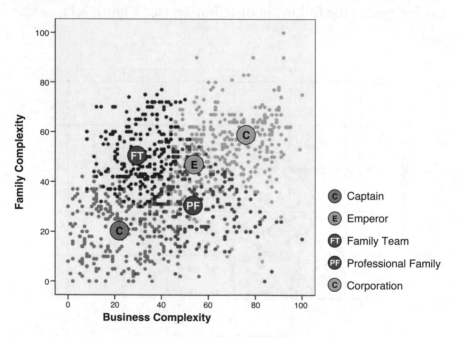

Source: Authors' compilation

Figure 3.2   Average complexity profiles of the family business models

- Family Team Model
- Professional Family Model
- Corporation Model

We have also clearly identified a sixth model, although we have no quantitative data for it:

- Family Investment Group

As can be seen in Figure 3.2, the average complexity profiles of the five types are notably different.

However, not all five types are so different in terms of degree of structure development, as we can see in Figure 3.3.

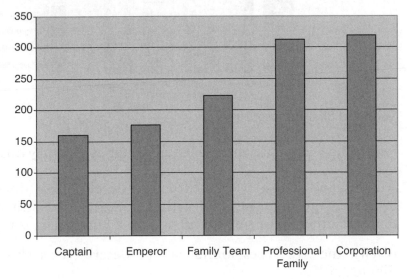

Source: FBK Database, 2007

Figure 3.3   Structure development by types of family business

Structure development

It is interesting to note that types of family business that are as different in terms of complexity as the Captain and Emperor Models have such similar degrees of structure development. Equally, the Professional Family and Corporation Models are very different yet have strikingly similar levels of structural development.

If we break down structure development into its various components, we find that the similarity between types is maintained.

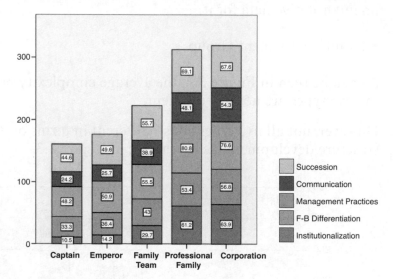

Source: FBK Database, 2007

Figure 3.4 Breakdown of structure by types of family business

All this goes to show that structure development does not necessarily go hand in hand with complexity, but rather that there are other factors determining how a family firm is run.

Briefly, the five types found can be described as shown in Figure 3.5.

Model	Characteristics
Captain	SMEs managed by the founder
Emperor	Businesses and families united by a leader
Family Team	Extended family working in a small business
Professional Family	Few family members engaged in professional management of a complex business
Corporation	Complex family governing a complex business
Family Investment Group	Family with varying complexities investing together

Figure 3.5 Characteristics of models

Captain Model

These are basically SMEs (small and medium-sized enterprises) ranging from extremely small companies (micro-businesses, technically speaking) to medium-sized ones. The average age of the business is 28 years, but as can be seen in the age distribution graph below, life expectancy drops significantly after the age of 20, and the presence of companies that have been operating for more than 40 years is marginal.

Frequency

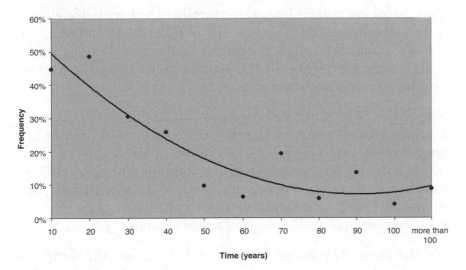

Source: FBK Database, 2007

Figure 3.6 Life cycle of the Captain Model[3]

Family complexity is also relatively low. The low business complexity is in some way duplicated in the low family complexity. The entrepreneur shares ownership with members of the family (mostly his or her spouse, and later on their children), and as a result the figure for the number of shareholders is the lowest of the five groups (2.6 shareholders on average).

These are 'founder businesses', i.e., they are the result of one person's effort, and usually last as long as that person has energy to spare.

Emperor Model

The Emperor Model is a different kettle of fish. The level of complexity is high in family and business alike. The average age of these companies in 41, and consequently they are led by either a rather senior founder or a still fairly young second generation.

This family complexity comes as a result of the passing of time. There are two generations working together, although power is in the hands of a single person who leads both the business and the family.

The shares are owned by several family members belonging to different generations. The average number of shareholders is 5.1, although they follow the family leader and do not exercise their ownership rights. In the second generation the average number of shareholders increases 78% to 9.1.

The degree of structure development is very similar to that of the Captain Model, which means that these businesses are run in a very similar way. The success or failure of the family business depends mainly on the abilities of one dominant person with high managerial discretion.[4] Hence the names of the models: a captain is someone who commands a simple unit, whereas an emperor wields power over a wide range of social systems.

As the frequency curve in Figure 3.7 shows, the Emperor Model is built over time. Frequency is very low at first but grows rapidly during the first 40 years of the life of the business, then drops dramatically.

This implies that it is a highly successful model for a cycle equivalent to one generation, but that it diminishes with the second generation as rapidly as it grew in the first.

The difference in complexity between the Captain and the Emperor Models is due basically to two factors: time and the resources of the family leader.

The passing of time brings an increase in family complexity. As the Emperor Model is on average 13 years older than the

Captain Model, family complexity is higher. At the same time, business complexity is also higher, since growth requires time, but all the more so because of the leader's resources. Thus, on average, we can say that the Emperor is more competent as a manager, or more growth-oriented, than the Captain.[5]

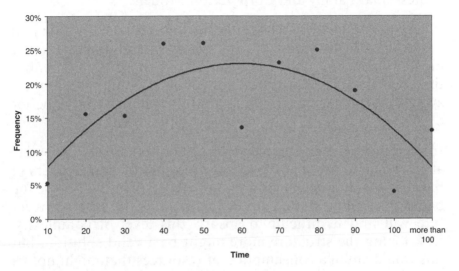

Source: FBK Database, 2007

Figure 3.7 Life cycle of the Emperor Model

Family Team Model

In this type of family business we find a feature that is unique to this model, namely that family complexity is greater than business complexity. The average number of shareholders is relatively high (6.5).

The disorder that can be created in the business as a result of family complexity would appear to be limited, as restrictions are applied to the entry of family members into the firm (only 36% of shareholders work in the business). This limitation is to some extent spontaneous, as the small size of the firm makes it unappealing for the professional development of many family members, who opt instead for a career outside the family business.

The differentiation between ownership and management incorporated into this model requires a structural development that is deployed as far as possible. As a result, its structure has a medium level of development, midway between the low level of the Captain and Emperor Models and the high level of the Professional Family and Corporation Models.

In comparison with single-person businesses (the Captain and Emperor Models), power is more evenly spread (higher level of institutionalization), there is greater family/business differentiation, which makes it possible to keep many of the shareholders away from management affairs, and communication is better developed, given the family complexity that exists.

In the future, family complexity is bound to increase considerably: suffice to say that the average number of shareholders in the next generation will grow by 48% to 9.5. This will cause the business to enter into a situation of risk, as the current structure will find it difficult to absorb this level of complexity. Developing the structure more might be a valid solution, but this would entail a consumption of resources that might not be available in this model (leaders' time, economic resources spent on consultancy, governance bodies, etc.).

Thus, in this model there are two main future alternatives to avoid falling into high-risk situations. One is to boost growth in

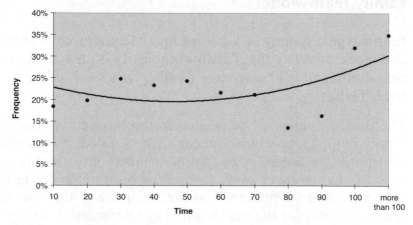

Source: FBK Database, 2007

Figure 3.8   Life cycle of the Family Team Model

order to have the capacity to develop an appropriate structure, and the other is to reduce family complexity by cutting down the number of owners.

The life cycle curve for this model shows a slight drop over the first 30 years, followed by a levelling out and gradual growth towards the end of the period.

Professional Family Model

The Professional Family Model has an inverse complexity profile to the Family Team. Business complexity is notably higher than family complexity. Businesses of this type have undergone a relatively high level of growth and development, and display a medium level of business complexity, practically on a par with the Emperor Model.

The great difference between this and the Emperor Model lies in how it is managed. Its structure is completely different. Growth and development have come not from one highly competent leader but from a well developed family business structure. Right from the first generation, the family opted for a less personalized management model.

The family is closely involved in management. This is the model with the highest number of family members in management posts (an average of 3.0), but these family members behave professionally, owing to the differentiation they have created in their family/business relationship structure.

The family is a managerial family: it is oriented towards running the business, but with a high level of sophistication in management and structure in general.

As can be seen in Figure 3.9, the frequency of this type of business grows slightly in the first ten years, then passes through a long period of stability and drops away over the last 40 years.

The small number of businesses that begin with this model suggests that it is not the best model for the start-up period. If we look at the rest of the graphs, we find that the Captain or Emperor Models might be more appropriate at start-up.

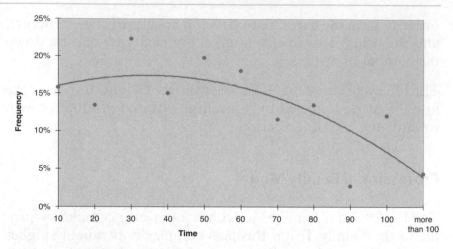

Source: FBK Database, 2007

Figure 3.9   Life cycle of the Professional Family Model

This should be food for thought for academics and consultants alike. It is important to avoid recommending family businesses to implement structures that are inappropriate for their complexity profile (i.e., oversized).

However, once the start-up period has passed, this model proves to be successful until increasing family and business complexity probably cause it to evolve towards the Corporation Model.

Corporation Model

The Corporation Model is the most developed, in several dimensions. It shows the greatest complexity both as a family and as a business, and is also the type with the highest average age (61).

The level of structure development is also the highest, although it is only slightly higher than the Professional Family Model.

As an indication of its high family complexity, the average number of shareholders is 13. Despite this, or perhaps because of it, it is the model that imposes most limits on family members entering management.

These are family businesses in which the family has evolved towards the ownership side differentiated from the management side. The presence, in some cases, of family members in top management is circumstantial. Those firms that are managed by family executives could easily evolve into firms with non-family executives, which are also included in this model.

The success of this model over time is incontestable, as a glance at Figure 3.10 will show. The passing of time makes this model the dominant one, because, if complexity increases, the other models either evolve towards this model or they tend to disappear.

In our opinion it is unnecessary to give concrete examples of firms for the reader to associate with each family business model we have identified. We think the reader will be able to identify firms that he or she is familiar with and that fit each model.

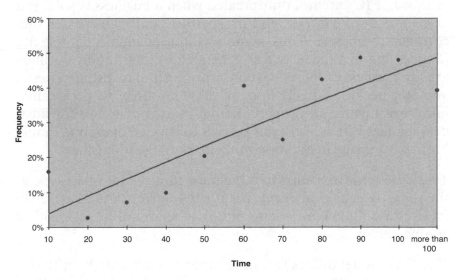

Source: FBK Database, 2007

Figure 3.10   Life cycle of the Corporation Model

Family Investment Group (FIG) Model

We have studied this model qualitatively but not quantitatively, and therefore we are unable to present data on it.

A large economic surplus is required for this model to occur. This surplus might originate from a family firm that is already operating, the sale of a firm, or even capital assets inherited from previous generations.

In a FIG, the family makes joint investments but does not take responsibility for the management of the businesses, and so the relationship between the family and its investments should be different from that between the family and its family business as such.

Typically, FIGs are created when the family is unable or unwilling to go through the various types of family firm described in this chapter and decides to sell the business. This sale generates a large economic surplus and the family decides to organize itself to manage these resources together.

However, FIGs are not only created when a business is sold, but also in cases of complex and prosperous family businesses that continue to operate. Thus, some medium or high – complexity families find that the resources generated by their family business are far in excess of their own consumption and investment needs and they decide to divert some of these resources to performing joint investment and property activities. It is common for business families with a history of success to have an operating family business or group in addition to their assets-based business.

This latter case amounts to a business family that possesses, at the same time, a family firm that it runs actively and also a FIG (real estate, financial assets, minority shareholdings in other companies, etc.).

The FIG model differs from the other models chiefly in that it is concerned with investment companies rather than operating companies. The fundamental difference between the two, for our purposes, is that the value of operating companies is directly related to the quality of their management; therefore, good management can lead to a major increase in value, whereas bad management can be a huge destroyer of value. In fact, this effect is becoming increasingly obvious.

In contrast, changes in the value of investment companies have more to do with the right or wrong selection of investments than their influence on the management of the businesses they invest in. To give an extreme example, if a family owns a building in a central street in any city, the value of that property will depend more on external factors than how it is managed. It is the same case as owning a small percentage of the family business and not being in the governance structure, or any other financial investment, as an increase in value will not depend on the FIG's management skills but other people's.

In the family's relationship with all the models described up to now, it was essential that the family should provide entrepreneurship and ensure the full functioning of institutions, especially the Board of Directors and the Management Committee. However, in the case of the FIG, the family's role should consist primarily in creating a favorable atmosphere for an ordered and prudent management of its investment portfolio. The FIG is a good model for preserving rather than for creating value. FIGs frequently offer their partners a range of services, such as filing tax returns, making tax payments, book-keeping for particular activities, insurance and so on.

Comparative analysis of the models[6]

Each of the family business models identified tends to be concentrated in a particular quadrant of the complexity profile, as we can see in Figure 3.11.

Four of the types (the Captain, Family Team, Professional Family and Corporation Models) tend to cluster in the four quadrants, without much overlapping. The behavior of the Emperor Model is different, as it occupies a central position overlapping basically with the Professional Family and Corporation Models.

From the structural point of view, as we saw earlier in Figure 3.4 (structure development bars), the five models could be divided into three groups:

The first group would contain those family business models that have a simple structure development. They are single-person models in which order emanates from one particular individual (the Captain and Emperor Models). The second group, with an

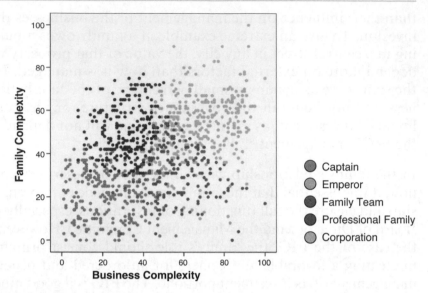

Source: Authors' compilation

Figure 3.11   Complexity distribution of the five models

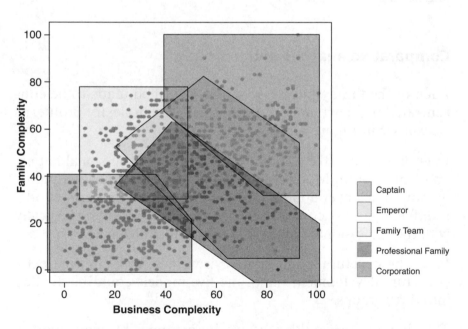

Source: Authors' compilation

Figure 3.12   Complexity area of the family business models

intermediate structure development, would comprise the Family Team Model.

Lastly, the third group would consist of those models with a similarly elaborate structural development (the Professional Family and Corporation Models), although they are two different types of business structurally, as we saw in Figure 3.3. They have the common denominator of a high structural development, but each model shows a different way of approaching the business. The first does so as a managing family, the second as an owner family.

Mindset and structure: how thoughts influence deeds:[7]

Our analysis of the different types of family business leads us to ask ourselves about the causes for the existence of these different types. We have already dealt with one of the causes: the complexity profile. Family and business complexity generates the need to create ordering structures to match that complexity.

However, this cannot be the only explanation, or even the main one in some cases. We have seen that businesses with very similar complexities (Figure 3.12: areas and complexity) can belong to entirely different models. The Captain and Emperor Models have different complexity profiles yet similar structures.

At the same time, the Professional Family and Corporation Models again have similar structures but different complexity profiles, with an important difference: in one the family dominates the management of the business, while in the other the family focuses on ownership.

The second explanation, beyond complexity, has to do with the influence exerted by our way of thinking about reality and how we act towards reality. The idea we wish to get across is that people's behavior is not only – not even primarily – the result of the reality surrounding them, but of the meaning they give it; how they interpret it. In other words, how thoughts influence deeds.

Thus, for example, a student failing an exam will not have the same meaning if he thinks he failed because the teacher dislikes

Figure 3.13   How thoughts influence deeds

him or if, on the other hand, he thinks the other students studied more than he did. If he relates the fact of having failed not to his own deeds but those of others (the teacher in this case) probably he will not feel the need to change the way he studies, but instead to pay more attention to his relations with the teachers in order to improve their feelings towards him and so avoid failing another exam. Therefore, his deeds will be aimed at improving his relationship skills in order to influence the teachers' deeds positively. If, on the other hand, he thinks his failure is due to lack of studying, he will concentrate his deeds on extending that task.

How the business is perceived, the ends that are pursued, the image of business development that is borne in mind; all these are essential aspects of the characteristics developed in the business.

Captain and Emperor Models (single-person models)

These two family business models share the same mindset, and consequently are managed in the same way, despite being different types of business.

This mindset rests on two main ideas:

- The family business is represented by a single individual. In this mindset, the business is an extension of a leader who does (or undoes) as he or she sees fit.
- Ownership and management are inseparable. In this mindset the value of the business is provided by its managers. Ownership is relatively 'accessory'. Hence the owners must manage the business. The separation of ownership and management is meaningless.

This mindset adopts the following characteristics in action:

Structure is focused on the entrepreneur. Order is imposed in both the family and the business by the dominant family member, who is usually the founder of the business. Structure is no further developed than the entrepreneur or dominant family member requires it to be.

The business is strongly dependent on the entrepreneur and his or her characteristics, motivations and vitality. Loss of vitality in the entrepreneur involves loss of vitality in the business.

Institutionalization is very low, as there is little sense in having a decision making body (the Board of Directors) with power over the entrepreneur in his or her own business. Nor is there any point in having a Family Council. A family constitution is more common, as it provides the opportunity for the entrepreneur to institutionalize his or her rules.

The family/business relationship revolves around the workplace. The family issues are who works and who does not work in the firm, and what their salary is. The component of ownership is practically absent.

Management practices are not developed to any great extent. The business shows the entrepreneurial development that the high managerial discretion of the entrepreneur allows. Quality of management depends, therefore, on the resources and skills of the entrepreneur.

Communication, as regards the Differences Management, tends to be fairly deficient, as the entrepreneur conducts relationships from a position of 'superiority'.[8] Differences are therefore often 'non-existent', because the entrepreneur's leadership prevents them from emerging.

Succession may be more or less prepared legally and economically, but it is difficult to prepare in management aspects, given the high dependence the business has on the entrepreneur. When he or she 'ages', the resulting frailty tends to be transmitted to the business. In the case of the Emperor Model, the lack of structure makes the entrepreneur's age an extraordinary structural risk factor. Succession is viewed as the replacement of the entrepreneur by one of his or her children, or else by more than one acting as if they were one.

As we mentioned earlier, the Emperor is unlikely to be able to duplicate himself within the same model. This may be obvious to an outside observer, but not to the Emperor, as his model does not allow him to see other models and realize the limitations it has when he weakens or dies.[9]

Professional family model

As examples of this model, we could mention a business run by a family (such as a hotel) or a professional activity carried out by a family (such as an administrative agency or a professional office).

The mindset rests on the following ideas:

– The business is at the service of the family. The business is a workplace for the family members, and its objective is to generate professional status and economic security for them.
– The 'value' of the business lies in working in it, and so everyone is welcome to work there. Not to do so implies not being interested in the family business and therefore not receiving income from it either.

The structure that goes together with this mindset is characterized by high development, maintaining the priority of the family in management and the limitations that its small size requires.

Here the business is not a game played by a leader, as was the case in the single-person models, but rather a family affair. As such, institutionalization is more developed.

However, family/business differentiation is as low as in the previous models. There is no point in building this differentiation, as the business is at the service of the family.

This lack of differentiation also means that professionalization of the management of the business and the structuring of information are both low. The policy is rather one of 'everybody muck in and it'll all work out'.

Communication, on the other hand, is much more developed, reaching levels close to the Professional Family and Corporation Models. The family's capacity for communication is one of the reasons why it has not yet choked the business. However, it is an undemanding sort of communication; as the family is given priority in decision-making, family agreements are reached more easily, although ultimately there may be a price to pay for the poor entrepreneurial development of these businesses.

Succession is developed to an intermediate level. Their capacity for communication enables these families to deal with 'difficult issues'. The priority given to the family also makes for an understanding relationship with family members who are being succeeded and allows the process to be made in a way that is comfortable for them. This takes its toll in the form of a lower capacity for regeneration in these companies, and therefore results in less development.

The mindset rests on the following ideas:

- The Professional Family Model breaks away from the concept of 'family equality', that is, family members do not necessarily relate to each other depending on their position in the family hierarchy. This means that the members of a particular gener-ation are not always equal and there may be differences between them.
- The family can therefore recognize that there are differences between its members, as a result of their skill profile, interests, life style and so on. The family can acknowledge differences without this meaning that anyone is better or worse in absolute terms. It is accepted that individuals have many facets, and that it possible to build by taking advantage of what each person has to offer.
- Another important aspect of this mindset, linked to what we have just said, is the differentiation between person and role. In this way, instead of 'being' the manager, for example, a particular person 'acts as' the manager. This enables one person to 'act as' several things in the same family firm, i.e., to play more than one role. Thus, a family member will play different roles when he or she acts as a company executive, a board member, and a Family Council member, for example.

The differentiation between person and role is related to the breakaway from equality. The members of the family can accept that the relationship between them is different depending on the role they play in each case. So they can relate as equals when they are in their role of owners but as superior and inferior when they are in managerial environments, for example.

In this mindset, the family has integrated the ability to impose limits on itself, as it is aware that this allows the business to develop more fully. These limits do not prevent the family from seeing itself as a managing family, that is, a family that must be capable of nurturing a quality professional to occupy the post of General Manager of the company.

Family/business differentiation is also notably developed. Work differentiation is important: for access to management posts in the business, promotion and remuneration, criteria of professionalism are used and standards are demandingly high.

Management practices are much more developed than in the previous models, as regards both practices as such and information and knowledge. It is interesting to see how, with completely different management practices from those applied by the Emperor, these two types of business have reached a very similar level of complexity.

Communication is likewise more developed than in the previous models, despite the fact that family complexity is notably lower than in the Emperor and Family Team Models. The mindset makes it possible to have in-depth conversations on a wide range of issues in a climate of mutual respect.

Succession is also more developed. This includes not only the more clear-cut aspects of succession such as partnerships, tax and wills, but also 'softer' aspects such as recognition of the skill profiles of different family members, transmission of entrepreneurship and so on.

Corporation Model

In the Corporation Model, the mindset is that of the owner family, unlike in the Professional Family Model, where we find the mindset of the managing family. This means that the family sees itself as responsible for the success of the company without a family member necessarily having to occupy the post of General Manager.

Thus, the General Manager is an 'employee', regardless of whether he or she is a member of the family; that is, someone who is paid by the owners to lead the company where the family wants it to go.

The family does not take on the need to manage the company, but it does take on responsibility for its good management, which makes it demand high standards from the management team. Thus, for example, it makes sense to replace a family executive if his or her performance is not good enough.

This mindset places no limits on structure development. So, for a corporation-type family, structure development can be as sophisticated as necessary, as long as there is the capacity to do so, without the family's way of thinking being an impediment to structure development. The limits are set by the family's competence, but not by its mindset.

Its structure is similar to that of the Professional Family Model. Thus, the level of institutionalization is high. It is slightly more developed in all its dimensions than the Professional Family Model. Nevertheless, institutionalization is rather more developed on the levels of management (Executive Committee) and governance (Board of Directors) than on that of the owner family (Family Council). This can be attributed to the poorer knowledge of the functioning of this body.

Family/business differentiation is developed in all its dimensions, but particularly so in that of Ownership Recognition. Within this structure, it is the owners who really have maximum authority, although they would do well to improve the Family Council Effectiveness in order to exercise that authority more fully.

Management practices are well developed, as is Communication, although in the latter more attention is paid to explicit statement of rules than to Differences Management.

Succession is also developed, but less so in the area of entrepreneurship than is the case with the Professional Family Model. It seems as if the greater distance of the family from management might represent something of a hindrance for the transmission of the entrepreneurial spirit.

4

Family business management

In this chapter the reader will be able to decide his or her future strategy for the family business, by weighing up the possibility of remaining within the current model or evolving towards another more suitable family business model. In the event of opting to evolve, we suggest the appropriate process of strategic change.

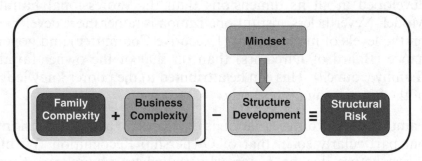

Figure 4.1 Influence of mindset on structure

According to the formula presented, the aim of management in the family business is to keep structural risk as low as possible. This involves making decisions about family complexity, business complexity and the development of the series of dimensions that make up structure. As we saw in the previous chapter, the mindset determines the possible courses of evolution that a family business can follow. For this reason, the management of the family business requires identifying the mindset that underpins it.

Definition of the problem: mindset versus structural problem

The relationship between mindset and structure development as identified in the various family business models is extremely useful both for the business family itself and for the professionals that advise the family.

Returning to the concept of the main lines of work towards which each family business model should be oriented, we see that there are two types of action to be taken:

• Developing the structure and/or
• Changing the mindset

Thus, for example, the line of work to be pursued in the Captain Model focuses on replicating the model. For this task, the existing mindset poses no hindrance; quite the contrary. The family's way of thinking is aligned with the proposed change. The future lies in the issue of structure, i.e., on being capable of finding a new leader with the right skill profile.

This is not the case with the Emperor Model. The model is not replicable, and therefore the future lies in a change of model and evolution towards the Professional Family Model or the Corporation Model. This requires an effort with regard not only to structure but also to the mindset.

The Emperor's mindset precludes the development of the structures inherent in these other two models. Institutionalizing, differentiating the family from the business, professionalizing management practices, developing communication and continuity: all this is incompatible with the mindset of a person who maintains the idea that all the business needs is a strong leader who will drive it forward.

In order for structure to be developed, this project has to be meaningful for the family. If the essence of the mindset is 'when the cat's away, the mice will play', then the only efforts that will be seen as worthwhile are those that enable the 'cat' to be more watchful or to be around more.

Therefore, the first effort the Emperor should make is in the area of the mindset, so as to be able to think using the ideas of differentiating between person and role, and that in the business his children do not have to be treated as 'equals'. Unless these aspects are incorporated into the family's mindset, any effort made towards developing structure will be in vain.

In the case of the Family Team, the 'problem' is basically structural rather than mental. Efforts should be directed at reducing family complexity, as an oversized family may end up choking the business. If complexity can be reduced it will not be necessary to change model, and a structural solution will be sufficient.

If complexity is not reduced in the Professional Family Model, in time the family will evolve from a managing family to an owner family; in other words, it will evolve towards the Corporation Model. This requires a change of mindset, in order to incorporate the idea that 'the General Manager (and obviously the rest of the managers too) is "employed" by the family'. This step is the only obstacle it has to clear in order to be able to develop the structure as far as the family and the professionals around it are capable.

In the Corporation Model, on the other hand, the main line of work should be aimed at developing communication. What is needed is not a change of mindset but an improvement in communication-related processes, skills and habits.

What is involved in managing the family business?

Managing the family business is about managing the firm's relationships and its ownership structure. To make a comparison with a listed company, managing the firm's relationship with the owners is rather like providing information, dealing with the media, keeping in touch with the main investors and so on.

However, there are certain aspects of managing the family/business relationship that differ from all other dimensions of business management:

- It concerns personal aspects of people's private lives.
- It requires relational skills.

- Actions take a long time to yield results.
- It is unlikely to succeed without an understanding of the mindset in which the business and the family are conceived.

Managing the operational or strategic aspects of the business basically means dealing with external, impersonal matters: processes, investments, operations, alliances, markets, clients, etc.

On the other hand, those aspects specific to the family business are much closer to the bone. Here we are dealing with people's future, their hopes, expectations, fears, loyalties, grudges, etc.

Handling these issues requires the ability to deal reasonably well with interpersonal relationships. Managing the family/business relationship calls for sensitivity to appreciate what elements are at stake.

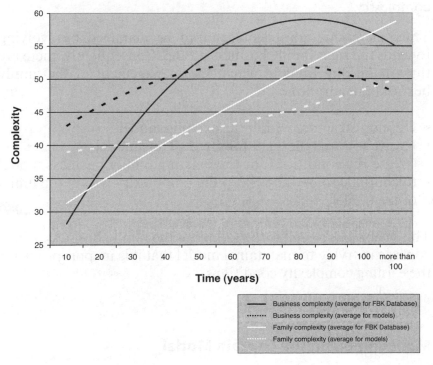

Source: Authors' compilation

Figure 4.2 Family and business complexity: FBK Database versus average for models[1]

Family business management is an ongoing process to develop the structure of the family/business relationship, although this process is punctuated with changes of model, that is to say, changes in the underlying way of doing things.

As can be seen in Figure 4.2, in the family business, family complexity (white line) and business complexity (black line) both tend to increase over time.

Figure 4.2 reveals that the increase in family and business complexity over time of the whole sample contained in the FBK Database is greater than the increase in complexities of the various models. This shows that in the lives of family businesses that survive there is an evolution towards models with greater complexity. Family businesses that survive change their mindset and their structure with an increase in complexity.

Thus, increasing complexity should be managed by evolving towards the right family business model. Consequently, there are three main directions in which the management of the family business can advance:

• Develop structure within the existing model
• Evolve towards the right family business model
• Create the conditions for the existing family business model to continue to be valid (keep the complexity within the limits of the model)

This enables us to define the failure of the family business, which consists in trying to maintain a model that it is inappropriate for the existing complexity conditions.

Management in the Captain Model

Family business management for the Captain Model should, first and foremost, match its basic characteristics: low family and business complexity. The stability of the model hinges on the figure of the Captain.

The Captain Model should work in three main areas:

- Professionalization of operations in keeping with the size of the business
- Succession management
- Preventing growth of family complexity

Professional management

Professional management is not out of bounds for small businesses. It is possible to be small and professional. Being professional in the Captain Model means:

- *Developing a clear strategy*

A clear strategic line indicates that the firm knows how it is going to compete, and what factors make it appealing to its customers. It is important to keep a close eye on the potential evolution of the sector towards new technologies, etc.

This does not necessarily require the strategy to be explicit (verbalized and possibly written). Many Captains have clear strategies that are emergent,[2] that is, that are not stated explicitly although the entrepreneur has them worked out in his or her head.

- *Create economic and administrative order*

This requires that the various operations of the business have the right economic register. This means proper accounting, calculating product costs, product and customer margins, etc.

Economic and administrative order is not unaffordable for a Captain business; indeed, the costs of not having it are much higher. The widespread availability of management software and the range and quality of professional services provided by administrative agencies facilitate matters in this respect.

Built rigorous processes

Professionalization also means reflecting about those activities that are carried out on a regular basis, with a view to setting up routines to make the work more efficient and of higher quality. In this way, the Captain's assistants will be in a position to participate in situations that arise within the defined processes.

• *Building account differentiation between family and business*

Professionalization means differentiating accounts, i.e., knowing when an expense pertains to and must be paid by the family and when the bill should be footed by the business. The same happens with the funds of the business. Account differentiation means that the family only receives income from the business through salaries and the payment of dividends.

Succession management

The Captain must address the issue of succession. As we mentioned in the previous chapter, he or she must seek another Captain in order to be able to bring about the transition.

This succession is prepared within a context of association between management and ownership; in other words, the person or persons who are prepared and willing to take the business forward will be those to give the business continuity.

The succession of the Captain should incorporate the need to prune the family tree, when the succession takes place within the family.

Preparing for succession forces the Captain to reduce the dependence that the business has on him or her. Succession is all about preparing people with sufficient energy to take over leadership. Captains often address this issue too late, which makes the handover from one to the other more difficult.

Businesses live insofar as they have the ability to evolve and adapt to new situations and competitive environments. Captain-type businesses are highly dependent on the Captain, and therefore the new Captain should be someone with sufficient entrepreneurial vitality.

Preventing growth of family complexity

The continuity of the Captain business depends on maintaining and developing in time the necessary resources to compete. In the Captain business, one of the main competitive resources is the Captain. The Captain usually concentrates a large part of the knowledge, relationships, leadership, vitality and strategic vision.

Figure 4.3 shows how, as business becomes more consolidated, the firm gains complexity (more sales, more products, more geographical areas). This may lead to an increase in family complexity.

The consolidation of the business may tempt the family to expand the number of owners in the future, some of the successors becoming only shareholders, without the need to work in the firm. This allows management professionalization and succession planning to have a positive effect on continuity, although a 'balancing loop' is generated along the way.[3]

Another negative effect for continuity in the Captain Model is related to time. Time affects family complexity, as ownership spreads from one or two people in the first generation to a larger

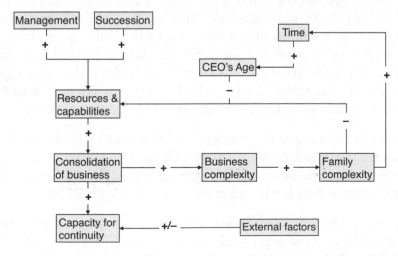

Figure 4.3 Factors affecting the continuity of the Captain Model[4]

number of people in the second generation, without taking into account the weakness that increasing family complexity brings to the business.

In view of all this, the Captain must prevent the passing of time or the achievement of minor successes in the development of the business from leading to an increase in family complexity.

In conclusion, family business management in the Captain Model should focus on professionalizing management practices, preparing for succession and preventing an increase in family complexity from ultimately choking the business.

Management in the Emperor Model

Managing the business according to the Emperor Model entails preparing the business for a different model from the current one. The Emperor is faced with the difficult task of activating change in a model which has served to bring success.

The Emperor Model is unlikely to be duplicable. The Emperor is a unique character who has developed a series of personal resources and capabilities over a long period. The structure he has created is an extension of him as a person. The repetition of the model, replacing one emperor with another, tends to be a failure, for three main reasons. First, it is difficult to find a new Emperor with similar characteristics to the old one. Second, in the improbable event that one can be found, the new Emperor will be unlikely to be able to coexist with the old one without entering into conflict. And third, the 'imperial' behavior of the new Emperor will not easily be accepted by the rest of the family.

Hence, in the case of the Emperor Model, family business management means evolving towards a change of model. The greatest difficulty does not lie in the new structure to build but in the transformation of the mindset that this change requires.

Managing the Emperor Model involves managing an evolution towards the Professional Family Model or the Corporation Model. For the purposes of the necessary change, evolving towards one or the other makes little difference, as they both require a major qualitative change, in the form of switching from a one-person model focusing on the Emperor to a model focusing on internal organizational structures.

As we have seen, the Captain and Emperor Models are very similar both in their mindset and in the structure on which they are based, although they are very different types of business with regard to their complexity. The Emperor is often tempted to understand the succession of the family business in the same way as the Captain does, i.e., repeating the model.

In the case of the Captain Model this is workable, but in the case of the Emperor Model managing in the direction of finding another Emperor is not usually possible. The Emperor needs to manage his family business by channelling it towards the Professional Family Model or the Corporation Model.

Overcoming the temptation to repeat the model is the first and biggest hurdle the Emperor has to clear. The aim is to manage towards abandoning the dependence the business has on him.

This means that the Emperor has to 'realize' that the model must get rid of him. It implies designing the future not in terms of 'who is going to replace me' but in terms of how to change the structure so that this can produce a new organization.

Our experience is that in most cases this does not happen, and Emperors wrongly channel their businesses towards repeating the Emperor Model.

In those cases when the Emperor is aware of the issue, his movements towards structural change should be strategic, and aimed at starting up a process that generates maximum development as naturally as possible, without the evolution of the model creating situations of disorder due to the abandonment of the old model before the new one is fully consolidated.

Structural change in the Emperor Model

Structural changes are processes that take time. A change of model such as we are concerned with here requires a long period to take root. It is quite reasonable to think in terms of ten years. An 'accelerated' process is less likely to succeed than one that respects the proper timing of things.

It is recommendable to focus change on the following lines of action:

1. Institutionalize gradually
2. Reach a family consensus to differentiate family and business
3. Incorporate or nurture professionals at the top management level
4. Create Top Management and occupy the post of Chairman of the Board
5. Treat the other shareholders 'as equals'[5]
6. Encourage entrepreneurial behavior in the next generation

Institutionalize gradually

The process of institutional development is a gradual process. Institutionalization is not about having or not having differentiated governance contexts, but rather to what extent those contexts work.

The Emperor should set up three main governance contexts: the Family Council, the Board of Directors and the Executive Committee. Only by creating these bodies will it be possible to start to bring about changes in the rest of the elements of structure.

As the Emperor makes no distinction between ownership and management, the Family Council provides the opportunity to try out this distinction. The Family Council basically serves two purposes. First, it allows the emergence of social leaderships[6] to complement the totalizing leadership of the Emperor. And second, it provides a start to sharing information and decisions with the family. This involves beginning to create relationships of equality[7] to which the Emperor is unaccustomed. The Emperor starts to inform and share decisions as a first development stage of the Family Council.

The Board of Directors should also play an important part. The Emperor should not concern himself about the functioning of the Board; just the fact of setting it up is enough effort for him. For the Emperor, creating a Board of Directors means giving up absolute power in decision-making. To this end, the Emperor should choose people he respects, and with whom he feels comfortable, to invite to be board members.

In its first stage, the Board should concentrate on sharing information and explaining its decisions and plans in advance, helping with comments and reasoning. This process will make it possible to introduce differentiation between management and governance, a difference that up to this time was non-existent in the mind of the Emperor.

This governance, of a low but very appropriate level of activity, has a second important utility: to initiate the process of explicit statement of strategy and professionalization of management practices.

If the Executive Committee does not exist the Emperor should create it, and if it does exist he should work to make it notably more functional.

The Executive Committee should be the key tool for developing General Management's vision within the management team. Emperors' management teams tend to be of a high quality, but not necessarily trained in teamwork, as they often act as 'support staff' for the Emperor rather than self-governing executives. The Executive Committee should serve to introduce General Management's vision among executives who may focus more on their particular functional area or business unit.

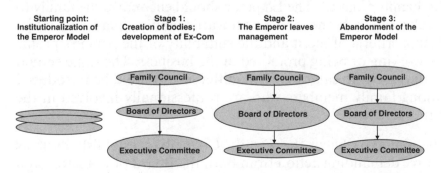

Note: surface area reflects the relative power (authority) of each body.

Figure 4.4   Institutional evolution of the Emperor Model

The development of a highly functional Executive Committee will eventually pave the way for the gradual retirement of the Emperor, who can leave General Management or become Chairman of the Board.

Figure 4.4 depicts the process of evolution in the institutional structure when the change of model is being proposed by the Emperor himself.

Reach a family consensus to differentiate family and business

It is in the Emperor's interest to initiate a process of conversation among family members in order for them to realize the need to differentiate family from business for the future success of the family firm.

The family should tackle this differentiate on three levels: job, ownership and exigency. The Emperor should initiate a process of transmission of responsibility for differentiation to the family group as a whole, although he can reserve the right to accept or reject the decisions reached by the family.

This means that the Emperor conveys to the family the responsibility for imposing limits on its members. The family must incorporate the need for self-limitation; otherwise it will represent a serious risk for the business. In the process of change initiated by the Emperor, it will no longer be the Emperor who enforces this differentiation. Rather, it will be everyone's responsibility.

The context in which this differentiation can take place will be the Family Council. The Emperor should encourage the family to break away from the tendency towards family equality by introducing criteria of merit and the suitability of the person's profile for working or being promoted in the business. The same should be the case with salaries, where differences should be introduced among family members who are professionally involved in the firm.

The Emperor helps the Family Council to establish itself as a force demanding action from both the Board of Directors and the management of the business. In this way, the family members should learn to demand results and to accept demands from others when they occupy positions of responsibility.

The Family Council should also serve for ownership to gradually occupy its proper place in the system. If the Emperor shares information, demanding systems are created from the top down, and family members are capable of discussing economic issues and transfer rights on equal terms, then ownership will gradually occupy the place it is due with the change of model.

Incorporate or nurture professionals at the top management level

It is in the Emperor's interest to develop management practices, in order to create less dependence on his personal intervention. This is not to say that Emperors do not have fully professional staff at their disposal, but often they lack sufficient freedom of action.

Figure 4.5 shows the centralized decision-making process.[8] Decisions are made by the Emperor himself, who performs his own diagnosis of the competitive situation of the company and decides on courses of action that his assistants will then have to implement. This system has the advantages of simplicity and speed. Assistants exist basically to put the Emperor's decisions into practice.

Professionalizing the business consists in enabling the executives to go beyond their tasks of execution and gradually incorporate tasks requiring decision-making.

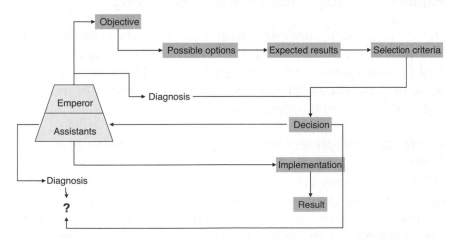

Figure 4.5 Centralized decision-making by the Emperor

Again, this is a slow process in which the Emperor should increasingly share diagnosis of the situation of the business with his team of assistants, in order to get a broad view of the firm's strengths and weaknesses and the nature of the resources at its disposal with which to compete.

Figure 4.6 presents the logic for conducting this professionalization process. The Emperor should discuss the situation of the company with his assistants regarding both its external competitive dynamic and its resources and resource base (diagnosis) in order to then set a series of goals for the assistants that will allow their full professional development.

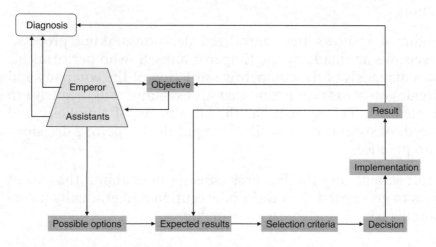

Figure 4.6   Decentralization in decision-making

In this way, systems are established that enable these professionals and their teams to learn and assess the quality of their decisions and the implementation of those decisions. This involves setting up management control systems, scorecards, competitor monitoring, competitive intelligence, etc.

Create Top Management and occupy the post of Chairman of the Board

With the structure development carried out thus far, it should be possible for the Emperor to take the crucial step of leaving the executive front line. The governance system should be institutionalized enough for him to go on to Stage 2 in Figure 4.4.

The combination of a Board of Directors with sufficient mileage and an equally developed Executive Committee allows the Emperor to leave management and the Executive Committee and concentrate on the Board of Directors. This is the first big step towards the Emperor ceasing to be the Emperor.

Treat the other shareholders 'as equals'[9]

The consolidation of the Emperor as Chairman of the Board should enable him to take the next big step in the change of roles, namely to introduce egalitarian treatment among the members of the family in the Family Council.

This is the time for the Emperor to forgo his predominant position in the Family Council and introduce relationships of equality. Both those members of the family group who possess legal ownership and those who possess psychological ownership should start to try out relationships of equality.

This is another of the indispensable steps in order for the following generations to assume the responsibilities of ownership, which they may have partially today, but which they will have totally in the future.

The Emperor maintains control of the company as Chairman of the Board, but he has now put into motion the structures that will ensure that his future decline and absence will not constitute a sea of troubles for the family business.

Encourage entrepreneurial behavior in the next generation

Although this point is the last on the list, it bears no sequential relationship with the previous points. It is developed beyond the scope of the business, and it is consolidated within the family itself.

The Emperor should act as a coach for the next generation, encouraging them to think of life as a universe full of all sorts of opportunities waiting for entrepreneurial vitality to put them into practice.

A large part of this responsibility should not fall to the Emperor alone but to the whole family. Families who develop enterprising behavior are very self-demanding families who orient their members towards achievement in an atmosphere of cohesion.

Developing enterprise in the next generation requires not just an instrumental approach but also the existence of values and culture in the family group.

Evolution towards a Family Investment Group

If the Emperor is unwilling to make the mental and structural change we have described above, or feels that he lacks the capacity or the skill to do so, in our opinion the only sensible option is to reduce business complexity, by evolving towards a Family Investment Group (FIG).

Evolving towards a FIG Model is much easier to achieve operationally speaking, but it entails the Emperor and family giving up leadership of their business projects. Evolving towards a FIG is tantamount to selling the operating company in order for the family to capitalize on the success of the Emperor Model, but avoiding the future risk inherent in it.

Selling the business is a relatively straightforward process, for which there are a multitude of specialists. However, it is very important how the family manages the liquidity generated through the sale.

Liquidity has the advantage that it allows the family to decide freely to continue as a business group. The family should decide whether it wants to keep up its business and investment activities jointly and set up as a FIG.

Ample evidence of the sale processes that unfold in the wake of the Emperor Model indicates that the continuity of the family's joint business activity depends to a large extent on whether they already had a FIG Model set up parallel to the Emperor Model. Emperors often develop, alongside their operating company, a considerable amount of assets in the form of properties, shares in listed (and sometimes non-listed) companies, funds of various types and new businesses set up by entrepreneurs they trust.

Emperors usually manage these activities within the Emperor Model. The Emperor decides the direction to be taken, partly

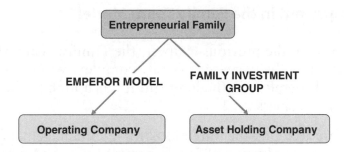

Figure 4.7 Mixed Emperor-FIG Model[10]

with the support of his team of advisers in the operating company. This generally means the financial manager, the business lawyer and the tax consultant, together with the asset specialists at the banks they work with, or directly with private banking specialists.

Some emperors have on occasions succeeded in separating these activities from the Emperor Model, and manage them as a FIG. When the FIG already exists, the family often remains united in its FIG activity, even with the injection of liquidity caused by the sale of the operating company.

In the opposite case, when the FIG does not exist previously, the family is unlikely to create it. Access to this high liquidity triggers a series of centrifugal movements that will be difficult to withstand without the previous existence of a FIG. The family is seized by a 'now-or-never' feeling that 'this opportunity' cannot be missed.

This is what tends to happen, as the combination of an operating company run according to the Emperor Model together with asset holding companies run as a FIG is unusual. The asset activities are usually also managed according to the Emperor Model.

As a result, selling the operating company is unlikely to evolve towards a FIG Model that would maintain joint asset management. It is usually accompanied by a reduction in complexity. This frequently involves the distribution of the assets among the various family branches, although within each branch these assets are often managed along FIG lines.

Management in the Family Team Model

As we saw in the previous chapter, the Family Team Model is threatened by the increase in family complexity that it incorporates, and therefore in the long run it has a high propensity to choke the business.

There are two possible directions for the management of this model: either reduction of family complexity in order to be able to successfully duplicate the model or evolve towards a Captain Model, or else growth in order to be able to move on towards a Professional Family Model.

The first management task in the Family Team Model is to realize that it is necessary to evolve in one of these two directions and that failing to do so means embarking on a process of steadily increasing instability and running the risk of seriously undermining both the competitiveness of the group and family cohesion.

Option of limiting complexity

Limiting family complexity means reducing the number of family members who hold shares in the business. This can be done through the purchase of ownership by the most business-minded branch or members of the family.

In this process it is important to avoid delegitimizing those family members who are less involved in the business or labelling them as 'uncommitted'; it should be seen by everyone as necessary for the future viability of the business.

The position of those who want to develop other business or professional projects is just as legitimate as that of those who want to carry on pushing the family business forward. Furthermore, the exiting of family members from ownership of the business is in fact an act of service, as it counteracts the increase in future structural risk.

The important thing about a family complexity reduction process is that it must be performed in such a way as to maintain, and even reinforce if possible, family cohesion and harmony. Likewise, the resulting ownership structure should strengthen the competitiveness of the business.

It is essential for the process whereby agreements are reached among the owners for the transfer of ownership to be fair and honest.[11] The focus must be on the clarity and transparency of the process, not on having necessarily to reach an agreement fixed beforehand in a negotiating position.

To this end, all family shareholders must form part of the pro-cess, independently of their degree of participation in man-agement. In the Family Team Model a large proportion of shareholders are not actively involved in the management of the business, and their views are seldom taken into consideration.

In the process of reducing complexity, the expectations, hopes and interests of the various members of the owner family must be defined. It is important to discuss which predominant alliance or alliances the family will feel most comfortable with, and what qualities will maintain or increase the company's ability to create value.

This process may seem arduous but it is vital, following the traditional premise in good negotiations of keeping the person and the problem separate,[12] in other words, being respectful to people, without that meaning having to tiptoe around sensitive issues. A person might love his brother dearly but that does not mean he is necessarily going to be comfortable sharing the dynamics of the business with him, and likewise they may have different conceptions about the business.

Option of growth

If the family chooses not to reduce or keep the same level of family complexity, the only possible option is to encourage the growth of the company to give it the capacity to develop a structure that will be capable of absorbing levels of family complexity that the Family Team is no longer able to absorb.

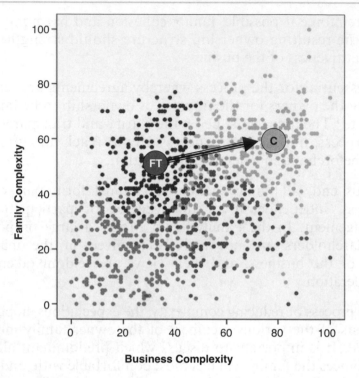

Source: Authors' compilation

Figure 4.8   Average complexity of the Family Team and Corporation Models

Evolving from the Family Team to the Corporation is not at all straightforward. First of all, the company will have to undergo major growth. A glance at the graph above is enough to see that the required growth and development of complexity are considerable.

The change of mindset that is necessary in the family is equally large. The family must stop seeing itself as 'the source of quality work for the company' and start seeing itself as 'a group of owners who give support to a particular business project but are highly demanding about results'.

This evolution is possible but there can be no doubt that it is uncommon, given the difficulties surrounding it.

Management in the Professional Family Model (PFM)

The Professional Family Model is a very solid one, but it has its weakness in the form of increasing family complexity. The rates of owner participation in the management of the business (76%)[13] are unsustainable if family complexity increases.

This confronts the PFM with two possible directions in which to channel its management: reduce family complexity or evolve towards a Corporation Model.

The increasing family complexity of the PFM causes structural risk by focusing the leadership of the business family on those individuals who occupy the senior management posts of the companies. This will have several effects.

First of all, there will be strong pressure to work in the business, and perhaps not only in senior management. PFM families are well aware of this risk, which is why they tend to place limits by fixing conditions of access, usually by means of a family constitution. Some frequent restrictions include having an MBA from a reputed business school; having successfully worked in another company or a similar job before; the existence of a job to fill; or preference will be given to a family member but with equal conditions to non-family professionals.

Although all these restrictions are sensible, reality tells us that when the time comes they are difficult to put into practice. As criteria they are too general to define who will occupy the senior management of the company, especially if we bear in mind the extremely long periods when the top executive is a family member.

The management of a business of a certain complexity, as is the case of PFM firms, is a responsibility that is too important to be decided according to such general criteria. Families who have developed this model tend to have competent offspring, so in the next generation there are usually several sons and daughters who consider themselves to be suitable candidates, and logically there are always several family alliances prepared to support one or the other.

The end result is often that a reasonably competent family member becomes General Manager, while other reasonably competent family members feel reasonably frustrated about not getting the job. They can put their misfortune down to not being children of the dominant family in the previous generation, not having the opportunity because jobs were already taken by the older members of their own generation, not receiving sufficient recognition or support from the family, and so on.

There is a potential risk of loss of family cohesion, as the family member who is in charge is frequently faced with more or less explicit internal opposition within the family group itself, and these historical differences often resurface in times of trouble.

As can be seen in Figure 4.9, the Professional Family Model maintains its frequency over the first 40 years, then gradually tails off. Family complexity remains constant, a very relevant point for purposes of management in this model.

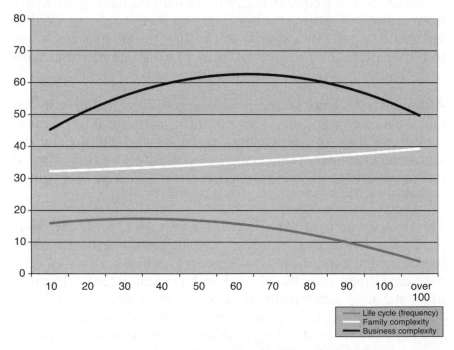

Figure 4.9 Evolution of the Professional Family Model

Business complexity follows an upward trend for the first 60 years, then shows a downward trend with a similar slope.

If we take the number of shareholders as our indicator of family complexity, we find that in this model the average is four, although it is expected to reach 5.7 in the next generation (a 44% rise).

Average family complexity in this model stands at 32.1. If this figure were to rise by 44% it would reach 46.2, which is clearly above the family complexity that this model is capable of absorbing (see white curve). One of the management options is to evolve towards a Corporation Model, which is capable of absorbing a much greater family complexity.

Another possible option is to duplicate the model on the basis of keeping family complexity low. The curves indicate that this option is possible, although there is a plainly visible decrease in frequency (and especially in business complexity).

In the hypothetical case of not being able to evolve towards a Corporation Model or reduce family complexity, there is only one valid option open to the family: to sell the operating company and so evolve towards a Family Investment Group (FIG).

As a result, family business management in PFM firms should in our opinion take one of the following three options:

- Evolve towards a Corporation Model
- Limit family complexity and duplicate the PFM
- Sell the operating company and set up a Family Investment Group

Option of evolving towards a Corporation Model

Evolving towards a Corporation Model means changing curve, changing life expectancy. It means switching from the downward life curve of the Professional Family Model to the clearly upward curve of the Corporation Model (see Figure 4.10).

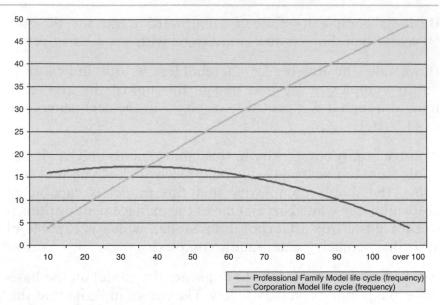

Source: Authors' compilation

Figure 4.10   Life cycles: Professional Family Model versus Corporation Model

This involves adopting a model that is much more sustainable in the long run, as it is capable of absorbing high family complexity and bringing about an increase in business complexity.

It also involves abandoning a business complexity curve that drops steeply after the age of 65 and adopting a slightly decreasing curve.

This evolution makes it possible to absorb the coming increase in family complexity (around 44%) without difficulty, as family complexity can rise from the dotted line to the solid line (see Figure 4.11).

Figure 4.11 shows that increasing complexity cannot be absorbed by the Professional Family Model but by the Corporation Model. Professional Family has to 'change the curve' into Corporation if it wants to absorb higher complexity.

Transforming the model involves a notable change in the way of seeing the family business. The family must abandon the idea that its contributions to the business are its capability in man-

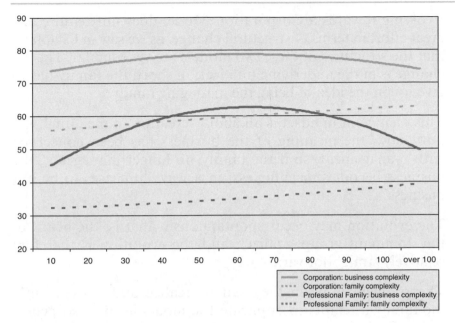

Source: Authors' compilation

Figure 4.11 Complexity evolution: Professional Family Model versus Corporation Model

agement, its commitment and its leadership skills; it has to turn towards an approach in which its chief value lies in being an owner family with the capacity to set up appropriate governance structures and to create a dynamic business capable of attracting managerial talent.

The managers are employees of the family, and therefore the family will not be concerned with managing the business but governing it. This is the gateway to a change of mental dimension for the family. The family must come to see itself as responsible for providing the company with quality managers, since it is answerable for the good governance of its family business.

This is not a simple evolution, as the PFM is the model that produces the highest level of satisfaction. The family feels competent developing its management skills and making a success of the business. As a result, the family tends to ask itself: 'Why change, if everything's going fine?'

Evolving towards a Corporation Model does not require any great effort in terms of structural change, as we saw in Chapter 3 that the structures of these two models are very similar. The big change is in the underlying mindset; in short, the family has to give up on the idea of being the managing family.

This change of mindset is all about 'creation of meaning'. Up until now, the meaning of the business has been concerned with management, so if the family no longer manages it, the business becomes meaningless; in a way, "it ceases to be our business".

The evolution may occur spontaneously, that is, the heads of the dominant group 'realize', and the evolution is therefore relatively straightforward.

The problem is when they fail to realize and consequently the family attempts to duplicate the model in the next generation. Such situations are often accompanied by 'dedicated investments'[14] by several members of the next generation. Some of them may have channelled their studies and their career in the expectation that the model will be duplicated, with a view to entering senior management of the business in the future.

Depending on what stage the business is in, this process may be even more advanced, with members of the next generation already occupying senior management posts in the business. This makes the change process more delicate, as it will have to be carried out in such a way as to cause the least possible damage.

Thus, there are two main tasks to be undertaken: changing the mindset and designing a non-traumatic structural change.

Changing the mindset

Changing the mindset means changing our way of thinking, changing our way of interpreting the things we see. Once, the son of an elderly couple who ran a well-known cake shop in Barcelona proposed a change to his parents. Considering that fewer and fewer people came to buy cakes on weekdays but sales at the week-end were holding up and sometimes even increased, and considering that the premises were quite large, he proposed they got some tables and a good coffee machine and so during the week they could serve morning and afternoon coffee and tea with cakes. His parents' reply was: 'We're pastry cooks, not waiters.' This meant that installing a coffee machine meant giving up their identity (as a pastry cook) they won't be able to make that change, because it won't have any meaning for them.

The mental difference (seeing the change as a loss instead of an element of progress) has to do with the 'meaning' the new project has for each person.

Designing a non-traumatic structural change

The evolution from the PFM to the Corporation Model does not occur in a vacuum; there is always a point of departure. The status quo created will be different for each person depending on the time in their life cycle. In most cases the family business will be run by a senior generation with a high level of competence and professionalization.

The key point for defining this process of evolution is the extent to which members of the next generation have already been incorporated into the business. They are usually highly skilled individuals occupying posts that are appropriate for them, since this model is characterized by a high degree of structure development, as we saw earlier.

The existing mindset tends to replicate the model with the idea that the 'most qualified' family members will join the firm. This will leave a group of family members who are less involved in it.

It is difficult for the family to realize that the group of family members chosen as 'competent' is unlikely to have the leadership of the previous generation, with a small family group and control over most of the capital.

Once the family has realized the importance of making the change of model, the main elements to take into account are:

- Age of those members who are professionally active in the business, in the generation in power and the next generation. Age allows us to approximate the stage at which each person stands in the life cycle. Depending on the stage in the life cycle, his or her relationship with the business will be different.[15]
- Level of irreversibility in their dedication to the business: to what extent they have career alternatives. The process of evolution will be simpler insofar as the family members working in the firm have career alternatives in the outside world.
- Economic situation of the players. Evolving from the PFM to the Corporation Model also affects the income of those family members who have been working in the business. The change should be as non-traumatic as possible in this respect.
- Social leadership[16] within the family group. Carrying through a change like the transition from the PFM to the Corporation Model demands a great deal of social leadership. Someone within the family group should take responsibility for 'moving' the whole family in the new direction and getting them to make individual sacrifices for the common good. This transition will not be possible without social leadership.

Reducing family complexity

Managing a reduction in family complexity in this model does not differ substantially from the process described in the above section on the Family Team Model, and we therefore refer the reader to that section.

Selling and setting up a Family Investment Group (FIG)

Selling the operating company and setting up a FIG might seem like an option to avoid, but this is not the case. What a family should really avoid is to create situations that it will be unable to resolve further down the line. For this reason, if a family judges itself to be incapable of evolving towards a Corporation Model and is either unwilling or unable to reduce family complexity, the one remaining option is to go for a sale in a beneficial situation.

Although it might seem paradoxical, selling may be the best option for continuity. Not doing so and duplicating the PFM with an increase in family complexity would be tantamount to letting structural risk increase notably. Selling would allow a simple change of model by regrouping as a FIG.

In operational terms, it is relatively easy to pursue this avenue, since the sale of a company is a process can be contracted out to a host of specialists in this type of operation. The difficult thing about this option is realizing that it is better – or less bad – than replicating the model with increased levels of complexity.

Management in the Corporation Model

The Corporation Model is the most highly developed of all, and allows the successful management of the highest levels of business complexity and family complexity.

We will not go into details about how this model makes it possible to manage business complexity. There are a wide range of tools, practices and techniques available to be implemented in the world of management. Many of them have been developed by corporate enterprises (understanding this in the currently accepted sense of listed multinationals), business schools and consultants. There is an ample bibliography on aspects of corporate governance, management of senior executive teams, creation of corporate structures (not to be confused with family/ business relationship structures, as discussed in this book), strategy-making, internal change and so on.

Therefore, the limits of business complexity that this model can handle are defined by the limits of our present knowledge of management. If we take General Electric as the prototype of a corporation with a highly developed management, there is nothing to stop a family business using the Corporation Model to reach similar levels of development.

We will, on the other hand, take the time to explore those management aspects that are more specifically related to family complexity. The Corporation Model makes it possible to introduce order into the highest levels of family complexity.

High levels of family complexity oblige the Corporation Model to attend to softer elements of structure such as the following:

• Communication
• The Family Group
• Entrepreneurial spirit
• Family Council

Communication

The increase in family complexity has brought an increase in differences, as explained in the section on family complexity. It is fundamental to develop the dimension of communication in order to introduce order into this complexity.

We have already explained in sufficient detail in the section on communication[17] which elements comprise communication as a dimension and how to develop it.

Family businesses that follow the Corporation Model should pay special attention to this dimension.

The Family Group

The family maintains its cohesion through its bonds of kinship. Family complexity, a product of the passing of time, gradually weakens these bonds.

As we saw earlier in the section on the Corporation Model, family complexity causes the original family to become weaker due to the appearance of priority loyalties to the nuclear family or family branch and the inclusion of numerous reference families[18] by marriage.

Loyalty to one's own family branch has a dynamic that weakens the family business enormously. Priorities gradually change and the objectives of reaching consensus for value creation in the business are transformed into defending the status quo or the privileges of one's own branch of the family. Expressions like 'We're entitled to one board member' become commonplace. Processes of loss of cohesion with the emergence of branches are slow, which is why this evolution goes unnoticed.

The importance of the above expression lies in what is meant by 'we'; who the speaker is referring to. When 'we' means one particular branch instead of the whole family, structural risk is growing.

One of the tasks that should receive close attention from a business applying the Corporation Model is that of creating an institution defined as the Family Group. This institution – understood as a shared mental construction – must have sufficient presence to constitute a current of predominant loyalties towards the family as a whole rather than one particular branch of it.

Just as the weakening of family cohesion is a slow process, so is the creation of the Family Group. Therefore, it is important to be aware of the inevitability of this weakening and the need for conscious action towards building cohesion in the family as a whole, beyond the natural loyalties of the immediate family.

Families acting within this model often perform joint activities enabling family members to share experiences and get to know each other better, activities related to the business (visits to plants, subsidiaries, etc.) and training activities. These may include courses prepared by the company executives themselves, customized programmes designed by business schools, or specific training programmes created within the Family Group itself. In connection with the latter type of programme, some families are institutionalizing these formats to create a 'family academy'.

In order to develop the concept of the Family Group, it is essential to keep the family informed about what is happening in the company: its situation, its challenges, its successes and its failures. 'To know is to love', they say, so it is important for the family to get to know the business, so that they will be capable of putting the good of the business – that is, the common good – before the needs and loyalties of each family unit.

This is a task that is frequently undervalued, and some more executive family members consider it to be rather a waste of time, whereas in fact it has an important function.

Entrepreneurial spirit

One of the key challenges of this model is how to maintain the entrepreneurial spirit. In the Corporation Model, the family is more distant from the nitty-gritty of business operations. The great family complexity and the high level of structure development that this requires diminish hands-on experience and the creative pleasure that it generates.

The development and sustained growth of a business demands an orientation towards innovation, towards risk, towards building 'the new'. This is easier to develop and transmit when one is directly involved in the creation, when it can be seen as one's own work.

The Corporation Model must strive to create different ways of participating in the undertakings of the family business. Some may be involved in these undertakings through the Board of Directors. But it is also necessary to create the conditions for the rest of the members of the owner family, from their positions in the Family Council or the Family Assembly, to be able to participate in these undertakings too.

The entrepreneurial spirit lies in the pleasure of belonging to a family that is capable of promoting an innovative company. To this end, it is important to create a family culture that gives meaning to business innovation. Families that succeed in transmitting these values always hold stories of the grandeur of what the family has been able to achieve.

The family legacy should focus on this pleasure of creating, rather than on duplicating a particular model of business, product or technology. The stories that the family must build should be centred on the importance of creation. Creation also means destruction. A family that is not prepared to sacrifice part of what it has built in order for 'the new' to appear will be unable to sustain the entrepreneurial spirit.

For this reason, a culture of some austerity is necessary. Without a certain amount of austerity in the family, allowing reinvestment and providing a means to overcome difficulties, the business will become dominated by the fear of losing what it has.

The fear of losing and the pleasure of creating are very different drivers in an organization. When a family conveys to its organization that it must be oriented towards the fear of losing, results may be good in the short term, but what appears in the mid term is conservatism and paralysis.

Family Council

The Family Council is the institution on which the Corporation Model should focus its attention. The rest of the elements of the system of governance are already developed in this model.

These families have learnt how to develop these other aspects from business schools, the world of non-family corporations and the various consultancies they come into contact with. Developing the Family Council is a more novel affair about which there is less experience available, yet it is fundamental in order to keep this model moving forward successfully.

The three aspects mentioned above in connection with the development of this model – communication, the creation of an identity as a family group, and the creation and transmission of the entrepreneurial spirit – require a fully functional Family Council.

Although we have already accounted for the Family Council Effectiveness, at this point we would like to highlight certain aspects that especially affect the Corporation Model.

Because of the high family complexity inherent in this model, there will be times when the Family Council will have to split into at least two bodies: the Family Council in the strict sense and the Family Assembly. In 25% of the Corporation Model businesses we studied, it was forecast that in the next generation there would be more than 20 shareholders. In such cases this split will be particularly important.

Management in the Family Investment Group Model

The FIG Model is suited to any type of complexity, whether business or family. It can be applied from the first asset investments made by a family to the management of large family assets. Investor AB,[19] belonging to the Swedish Wallenberg family, is perhaps one of the prime examples.

Managing a Family Investment Group involves dealing with the following aspects:

- Managing family cohesion
- Developing the right structure
- Managing the degree of family participation
- Defining the type of activities to perform and services to provide for the family

Managing family cohesion

The FIG is a model that lends itself easily to being divided up without very obvious losses of value. Shares, financial assets and sometimes even properties are easily distributed among the various members of a family.

Keeping the family united around a FIG demands a conscious decision by the family to the effect that it wants to maintain the management of its assets (or part of them) jointly. This requires the family to feel that staying together has two types of advantages.

The first advantage is that of size. Together, the family can face larger projects, stand out from the crowd as a possible investor, meet the costs of more skilled teams of professionals, develop a wider range of services for the partners, and so on.

Secondly, staying together involves building an identity as a business family around the idea that the FIG is a family business too. This is particularly important in cases when families sell their operating companies and come to have large amounts of liquidity at their disposal.

In such cases, families have a decision to make: whether to distribute the assets among the various family members for each to manage independently, or to manage them jointly through a FIG.

In the not infrequent event of the sale having come about as a result of loss of cohesion in the family group, it will be pointless for the family to set up a FIG, as the cause (whether explicit or implicit) of the sale was precisely the need to separate.

When the sale occurred for some other reason – strategic reasons, or an 'irresistible' offer – setting up a FIG is an alternative that the family should consider. The previous existence of a FIG will make it easier to develop this dimension, as we will explain in the section below.

A family's decision to stay together as a FIG and transmit these assets to the next generation has more to do with the component of family cohesion than that of economies of scale.

Although economies of scale exist and are important, they have nowhere near the sufficient strength to make a family with low levels of cohesion decide to stay together. It is family cohesion that enables a family to see an opportunity in the economies of scale created by the fact of staying together.

Developing the right structure (family office)

The FIG requires the development of a qualitatively different structure from that of operating companies. This structure is usually provided by the family office.

The family office is the management unit of the FIG. It dates back to the great industrial assets generated in the late 19th and early 20th centuries in the United States (Carnegie,[20] Hanna[21]). Despite its long history, the family office was not fully developed until the 1980s, with the increase in the personal fortune of a number of families throughout the world. These families' approach to how to manage their assets led to the establishment of the family office as a family asset management structure.

The structure of a FIG can vary greatly, from an administrative agent managing a small portfolio of assets to a sophisticated family office such as that of the Pitcairn family[22] or a powerful investment arm such as that of the Wallenberg family. One of the most outstanding FIGs in Spain is that of the March family (Corporación Alba).[23]

In the structure of a FIG the institutional dimension is important, but much less so the rest of the dimensions that make up structure.[24] The model is less relevant.

Family/business differentiation is less important, as we will argue in the following point, since there is little opportunity for the family to damage family assets.

Professionalization is relatively easy to acquire, as management of this type of business is a commodity that if necessary can be contracted out to various types of agents who provide this service for third parties, such as investment banks, multifamily offices or family offices that open their services up to other families close to them.

Similarly, the development of communication is less crucial, as the family is bound together by its concern with assets but not with the management or governance of operating companies.

Succession too is more straightforward. Here the family is dealing with ownership succession, not management succession. Even in those cases where management succession is affected, the problems surrounding that succession will be few.

The only dimension in which some development is necessary is institutionalization. The Family Council must be developed, although not to such high standards as in operating companies.

The Board of Directors should also function differently depending on the complexity of the FIG. It is advisable to include an external board member. This could range from an administrative agent, in the case of a low-complexity FIG, to a recognized expert in the field.

Managing the degree of family participation

The FIG Model is much more benevolent with the family than the Professional Family or Corporation Models. Generally speaking, the family can occupy the management and governance posts of the FIG without this jeopardizing the viability of the group.

The FIG will develop more or less depending on the skill and commitment of its managers and the structure that is created. These factors can have a positive affect by creating added value, as we mentioned earlier, yet are unlikely to destroy value.

As the model does not generate systems of limits for the family, the family itself has to define them. One of the big issues that the family has to decide in a FIG is the family's degree of participation in the business.

The FIG can be used to create jobs or management positions for the family, to a greater or lesser extent depending on the size of the business. The family can also occupy governance positions. As we will see below, a highly developed Board of Directors is not necessary, and this means that several family members can occupy posts in it without the requirements of the boards of operating companies.

The FIG can be used by families combining different dominant orientations (protective, venture-driven and financial).

Defining the type of activities to perform and services to provide for the family

Managing a FIG involves deciding and developing the range of activities the FIG should perform and what services it should provide for the family.

FIG activities usually start with property management, as a result of the separation of the firm's property assets, which are often held by companies other than the operating companies. Later on, these property investments tend to expand to other investments that are unrelated to the core business and incorporate financial investments. FIGs usually start to build their activities on these two pillars, property and financial management.

Once a FIG is equipped with a structure in the form of a family office of some importance, more sophisticated activities tend to appear such as buying shares in other companies. When these other companies are newly created we use the term 'seed capital'. When they are already operating but need capital to grow we refer to 'development capital'. And when these investment and divestment activities are performed using systematic and professionalized methods they are called 'private equity activities'.[25]

Investment activities in companies for their creation or development take on special importance when support is given to the undertakings of family members. In this case the FIG serves to give backing to the more enterprising members of the family, and constitutes a partner for an enterprising family member.

Family offices usually provide families with four main types of services:

- Counselling (financial, tax, legal, property)
- Management (insurance, company administration, purchasing)
- Other services (purchasing, IT, telecommunications, management of purchasing, events, trips, etc.)
- Training and development (courses, training plans, coaching, etc.)

Mixed models

Often the family does not own one single business but rather what is known as a 'family business constellation'. In these cases it may be perfectly feasible for the family to manage its various activities applying different models.

The commonest types of mixed models are when a distinction is made between value creation activities and value preservation activities.

It is highly recommended that this differentiation be made from a position of some business complexity. Therefore, it makes sense to combine a FIG Model with Emperor, Professional Family or Corporation Model businesses.

If the family business cluster differentiates between these two types of activity, both types of business will develop better. Developing a branch dedicated to preservation allows the family to take more risks in the branch aimed at creating value.

Family businesses often have a multitude of assets, basically property, that can be segregated from the operating business according to a FIG logic.

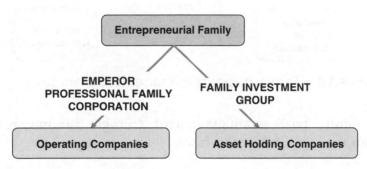

Figure 4.12   Mixed models

Family business management triangle

In the above sections we have presented the evolution that can lead on from each model, which is the most suitable depending on the complexity, and how these evolutions should be carried out.

All these possible courses of evolution require effort to be focused on the following dimensions:

- Change of mindset
  Some situations require a change of mindset to allow the evolution of the family business model (transition from the Emperor to the Professional Family Model, for example).
- Limitation of family complexity
  Complexity can be prevented from increasing or made to decrease, in order to be able to duplicate the existing model or evolve towards a model that only admits lower complexities than at present (when duplicating the Professional Family Model, for example).
- Structure development
  Structure can be developed as proposed in this chapter, if the existing model allows its development to match the existing complexity.

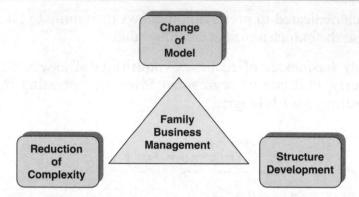

Figure 4.13   Family business management triangle

The family business management triangle summarizes our proposal as set forth in this book.

CONCLUSIONS

In this book we have related in detail the different perspectives from which family business has been studied. Each of these perspectives has added new elements to be taken into account in its development.

Our contribution to these perspectives has been to focus on the family/business relationship, describing the notable extent to which this feature pervades both the business and the family. We have chosen the concept of complexity as the key dimension accounting for the series of interactions that occur between the family and the business.

Complexity embraces a great number of highly diverse elements, interwoven and interrelated, affecting one another in such a way as to increase the number of possible behaviors, reactions, evolutions and processes. Complexity presents us with a future perspective based on uncertainty.

Therefore, when we propose approaching the business family in terms of complexity, what we are actually proposing is to observe the family in its growth process, the progressive increase in the number of members that comprise it, accepting that each new member brings his or her interests, aspirations and way of thinking and feeling about the business. The sum total of all of them, entwined within the concept of the family, will act in one way or another on the business. Unless it is properly channelled, this influence will cause disorder. Consequently, structures should be created to order and channel the family's intervention in the business.

Similarly, as the company grows, it too increases its complexity. It contains more elements to be taken into account; a larger number of interdependent processes. Action without regulation spreads disorder. Again, structures are needed to regulate processes, delimit responsibilities, and channel flows.

Structure is thus the core concept whereby we gain an advantage over uncertainty. By regulating and setting forth the way things work, we increase the levels of stability and control of both complex systems: the family and the business.

Structure is the pointer of the scales that can offset risk. Risk comes from the certainty that the greater the complexity, the larger the number of events that will arise: events that we cannot predict individually but we know will happen.

We dedicate considerable space to describing the different variables, which are statistically significant in the family/business relationship. Establishing order is a slow and gradual task requiring attention to overlapping areas of influence. Hence the detailed description of structure to be found in the annex.

Lastly, models are presented in an attempt to group together and understand the set of elements at stake. Given that there are multiple levels of complexity in families and businesses alike, we use models to try to describe general typologies with which family businesses can be compared.

By analyzing the various family business models, we can also depict possible future scenarios and design the transformations that need to be made in order to integrate the predictable increases in complexity.

On top of the construction of the different types of family business, a new aspect is added that does not form part of the Family Business Management Formula: the mindset. The mindset is the representation that each person makes of a given reality. Our mindset brings together our particular way of thinking about the world; our values, our beliefs. When we talk, in this case, about the family or the business, we are doing so from our mindset, and when we communicate with others we are interested in sharing these points of view.

The possible differences in the mindsets of family members regarding the business are a very serious matter, as they can easily lead to major misunderstandings and disagreements.

To conclude, the figure that closes Chapter 4 sums up the three main concepts that in our opinion should be taken into account in family business management:

The level of complexity that is going to be generated or that we are prepared to allow; unless we counteract it by reinforcing the structure, there is a risk of the business becoming unstable and entering into a process with unpredictable consequences.

Structure development, managing each and every element that enables us to progressively adjust the relationship between a family and a business, which is made more complex by the passing of time.

Change of model, as family business management is not a seamless process; on occasions it is necessary to make an important qualitative leap that requires the family to change their way of thinking about the family business.

The structure of the family/business relationship should be modified by dealing with the various dimensions of management. Thus, by influencing these dimensions, we change the relationship between the family and the business.

In the interests of an easier understanding of this book, the details of these management dimensions have been taken out of the main body of the text and included in the annex, in view of the fact that they are rich in shades of meaning and depth of content. In this way, the interested reader will be able to gain detailed knowledge of all the resources at his or her disposal to provide the right structure for the family/business relationship.

FBK-Diagnostic, available at www.fbkonline.com, provides a real-time assessment of the complexity and the status of the family/business relationship in each particular case, together with a suggested line of specific action to take.

Existence of institutions

The governance of the family business has traditionally been associated with three different bodies (Family Council, Board of Directors and Executive Committee), each with its distinct functions (to govern the business family, govern the business and manage the business respectively).

The family business is created out of management. An entrepreneur creates and develops a business. He or she is usually its driving force, its soul, its chief executive and also its owner. Decisions as to how the family should be related to the business are made depending on the circumstances as the entrepreneur sees fit.

The same happens with the governance and the management of the business. In businesses of this sort, normally no distinction is made between ownership and management. The entrepreneur makes decisions in conjunction with his or her management team, and when in doubt will ask a consultant or someone trusted.

The creation of a Family Council represents a qualitative change. It means that decisions concerning the business family are no longer made by the entrepreneur alone, but are the fruit of conversation, and perhaps agreement, among the influential members of the family as a whole.

The same can be said of the Board of Directors. Its creation implies a differentiation between management and governance. Strategic decisions and responsibility for the progress of the company are no longer solely in the hands of the entrepreneur, but rather are taken by a joint body. It means that the top executive, whether this is the entrepreneur or someone else, cannot run the business and make decisions as he or she likes, but must discuss them with the board, whose job is to approve them and account for the outcome.

The creation of a Executive Committee also represents a change in the institutional structure. Although the ultimate responsibility for management continues to lie with the top executive (whose job

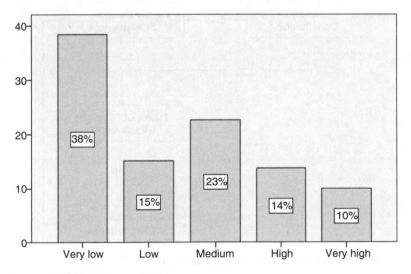

Source: FBK Database, 2007

Figure A.1   Existence of institutions

may go under the name of CEO or General Manager), the creation of a Executive Committee implies the existence of a group of senior managers who, regardless of their functional position in the business, run the company jointly.

The development of the Spanish family business in relation to this dimension is shown in the graph below. It can be seen that only 24% of these firms can be regarded as having a high or very high level as far as the existence of governance institutions is concerned.

Functioning of the institutional structure

Taken as a whole, these governance bodies are important as an institutional structure that goes beyond the individual functioning of each of its elements.

As can be observed in Figure A.2, the functioning of each body is strongly determined by that of the rest.

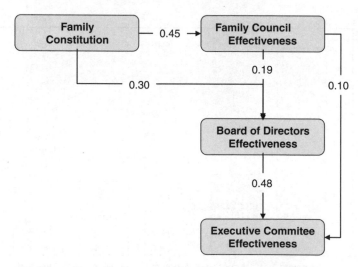

Source: *Radiografía de la Empresa Familiar Española, 2006*

Figure A.2   Effect of the institutionalized functioning of the governance bodies

The Family Constitution (set of rules) enables the Family Council to function correctly and prevents the family dynamic from 'invading' the Board of Directors. Under these circumstances, the Board of Directors can perform its governance function better, as it is not distracted by family affairs.

It is clear from the figure that good governance has an important impact on the Executive Committee. A good Board of Directors stimulates the development of the management team enormously, causing the Executive Committee to function notably better. The figure also shows that the Family Council encourages company management to have a more professionalized behavior, again leading to a better functioning of the Executive Committee.

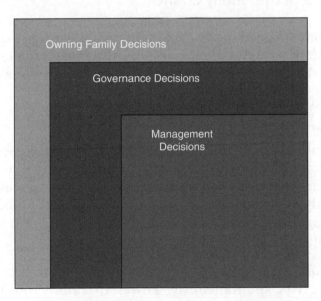

Figure A.3   Decision-making hierarchy of governance bodies

Family Council effectiveness

The better each management body performs its function, the more institutionalized the decision process will be.

This is why we talk of functioning. A Family Council that exists formally but hardly ever meets, or has no information or authority, is not the same as one that is really fulfilling its function.

All the members of the business family over a certain age should have a place in the family business. By 'place', we mean a 'social place', a way of forming part of the family business, of belonging. Often there is only one way of belonging, namely to work in the business. Those who do not work in it are outsiders; they do not belong.

Everyone should have a place, but it should be a functional place, that is, a way of participating that helps to achieve the ends of both the family and the business. Being in the Family Council is an excellent way of taking part in the family business.

Functions of the Family Council

The Family Council has five main functions. They are concerned with authority, the socialization of its members, cohesion and vitality, the defining of rules and limits, and representation or status.

Exercising authority

The Family Council represents the ownership, and as such it is the highest level of authority. It must decide where to set its limits as owners; in other words, to what extent it wants to exercise authority directly and what decisions fall to the Board of Directors and the management team. If the Family Council takes on too much direct authority, it is very likely to be incompetent.

As a result it is necessary to expressly build a hierarchy, which seldom exists spontaneously. Power in family businesses is usually in the hands of management, as management is the origin of the business. The business grew and developed in the early days due to its good management, not due to its good exercising of authority. Value lay, therefore, in management and not in authority.

One of the functions of the Family Council is to change the power relationship by giving power to the owners so that they are hierarchically superior to any other decision-making person or institution in the family business. This requires the role of the owners to be defined.

In the first generation, power is in the hands of the founder as the business leader. His leadership is based on management, on having been able to envisage a project and put it into practice. In the transition to the second generation, the founder attaches little importance to ownership; his children hold it because he has granted it to them.

This point of view is conveyed to the second generation, and so once again power is in the hands of those family members who run the business; they do not submit to the authority of ownership, which presumably encompasses both managing and non-managing family members. The tool for beginning to invest ownership with power is the Family Council.

This authority should define how power is distributed among the family members, what governance bodies will exist, who will be in them, who will work in the company, in what conditions, and so on. It is responsible for defining how the family is going to obtain income from the company, i.e., who will receive a salary and in what conditions and amounts, and what dividends will be paid.

The Family Council is responsible for appointing the Board of Directors, by defining which family members should form part of it, and which positions on the board will be set aside for non-family, whether in the form of senior management or independent directors.

The Family Council must give the Board of Directors a 'mission', that is, a set of coherent objectives with the firm's raison d'être for this family. The Board of Directors must attend to this mission, and is accountable for its accomplishment. In turn, the board will do the same with regard to the top executive and the Executive Committee, i.e., limit its own sphere of influence as the Board of Directors and give the top executive a mission and sufficient room for manoeuvre.

Lastly, the authority of the Family Council should be manifested and exercised in the face of unforeseen situations. The Family Council will have to deal with the series of unforeseen situations that will undoubtedly arise (growth opportunities, changes of strategy, contingent events, deaths, family crises,

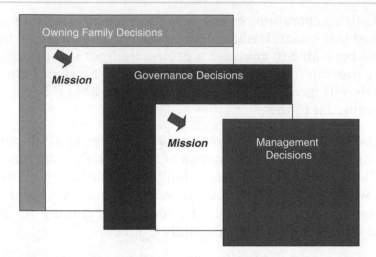

Figure A.4 Delegation of decision-making by governance bodies

quarrels, etc.). Some of these unforeseen situations will be resolved directly by the Family Council, whereas in other cases it will accept or reject the proposals made by the Board of Directors.

Socializing

The Family Council is a tool enabling the members of upcoming generations to get to know what it means to be part of the ownership of a family business.

The Family Council facilitates the socialization of young family members from post-adolescence onwards. It is a place where the young learn to feel and enjoy the business, exercise the responsibility of ownership, take risks and maintain confidentiality, i.e., what is discussed in the Family Council is not to be talked about later when out with friends. The young learn that being 'wealthy' is very different from being one of the owners of a business with a certain value.

Socialization is also about transmitting values and ways of seeing the world. The entrepreneurial spirit is also transmitted in the Family Council, although not only in the Family Council, as with the aspects mentioned earlier. This does not mean that all the family members are leading a business project (perhaps not even one of them, in the extreme), but it does mean that the family takes pleasure in it and recognizes the merit of the entrepreneurial developments.

The function of socialization also contains a component of training. Socializing in ownership involves ensuring that all the members of the shareholding family have sufficient knowledge to understand the vectors of value creation in a business, and to understand its basic financing by grasping the broad concepts of management.[1]

Representation and status

Typically, there are two positions with regard to the family business: 'being in the company' (i.e., working in it) and 'not being in the company'. However, it is important to extend these options and open up a wide spectrum of different ways of forming part of the family business.

In a family business of some complexity and considerable size, it is likely that not all the members of the family will participate on a managerial level.

The complexity of the business causes it to expand its influence on society into other areas such as cultural, civic, scientific, sporting and welfare activities, through foundations or other types of institutions, thus reinvesting part of its profits and carrying out socially valuable initiatives. Belonging to a business family may also be a way of accessing another type of collateral activity concerning the representation of the business in its social environment.

It is the responsibility of the Family Council to represent the family as an institution in the social milieu in which it moves.

Encouraging cohesion around the entrepreneurial spirit

In a family business, family cohesion should arise through the construction of a common project with the ability to appeal to the will of individuals.

The Family Council should create a sense of belonging and a pride in that belonging. The sense of belonging is an important element for any human being. Forming part of a business family is an element of identity for the family members and confers social status. When a family sells its business and chooses not to continue as a Family Investment Group, its social prestige as a family diminishes very rapidly.[2]

This cohesion generated by identity should be built around the idea of enterprise and creation.

Cohesion is also achieved through the information and knowledge that the family members have of the business. 'To know is to love', and knowing means being up to date with the various activities, projects and challenges in which the family group is involved.

It is also important to share information about the various members of the business family and their hopes, interests, personal situation, economic needs and so on. In other words, information about the differences among them should be shared and made explicit.

This function of encouraging cohesion and dynamism involves developing the ability to hold an ordered conversation and define moments, times, places and manners for dealing with each of the issues that each member of the owner family wishes to raise.

Creating limits and rules

The Family Council also has the function of setting limits to the family's intervention in the business. The Family Council is the place where the family starts to impose limits, in most cases first of all in economic and financial issues (salaries, dividends) and employment (who works in the family firm and under what conditions), and eventually working on more sensitive issues such as power, ownership and management succession, and the mission of the family business.

One commonly used way of imposing explicit or implicit limits in family councils is to draft a family constitution. The family constitution is a useful tool, although in some countries, as Spain, it has been used in excess, having been applied in pursuit of goals that it is incapable of achieving.

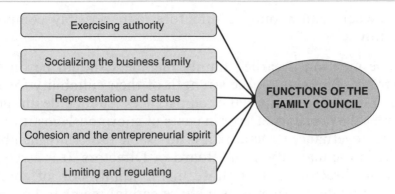

Figure A.5   Functions of the Family Council

Summary of the functions of the Family Council

As we will see presently, it is far from indispensable for all family businesses to have a highly functional Family Council; the council should match the need for order as required, which means that in each case it will depend on family complexity.

Board of Directors effectiveness

The Board of Directors is a governance body that the family business has in common with companies possessing other forms of ownership. Listed companies with a dispersed shareholding, venture capital firms, cooperatives, mutual organizations (friendly societies, savings banks), companies owned by institutions (foundations, NGOs) and public companies all have – or ought to have – a Board of Directors.

Composition and dynamic of the Board of Directors

No sufficient agreement can be found among specialists as to the correct composition of a firm's Board of Directors and the ideal number of members. In this section we will give our opinion, which is based on the literature, our research and our experience.

A Board of Directors should have few members: from four to seven, depending on the level of business and family complexity. The composition should be mixed, including members of the owner family, outside directors, and possibly company executives.

As we mentioned earlier, family members should be on the Board of Directors on the strength of their suitability for the job. Except in very special circumstances (sudden death, geographical dispersion, etc.) or in cases of enormously institutionalized governance structures, it is advisable for family members to be in the majority in the Board of Directors. It is essential that no director (neither those in the family nor, of course, those outside it) behaves as a share-capital member, i.e., as a member who represents the owners who named him and therefore owes allegiance to them. The directors should be appointed by the Family Council as an institution, and should owe allegiance to it.

As can be seen in Figure A.6, most Boards of Directors are made up exclusively of members of the family. 'Family' Boards of Directors are less functional than those that include directors from outside the family.[3]

The top executive should, of course, participate in board meetings, either as a company director as such (managing director) or as a non-member. In some cases it may be recommendable for certain other executives (e.g., the financial manager) to belong to the board in order to guarantee that the board has sufficient information.

External members are a fundamental part of the Board of Directors. We recommend their presence for a number of reasons. First of all, the presence of outside directors enables the board to take on a dynamic befitting a Board of Directors and avoid the

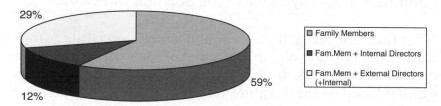

29%

12%

59%

☐ Family Members

■ Fam.Mem + Internal Directors

☐ Fam.Mem + External Directors (+Internal)

Source: FBK Database, 2007

Figure A.6   Composition of Boards of Directors

discussion of subjects that are more the jurisdiction of the Family Council or the Executive Committee. Secondly, they are a great way to introduce valuable skills into a board and so into a business. It is advisable to define the profile of the members with an eye to the needs of the company at the time. The general philosophy is to look for people who have 'already been' where the business wants to go.

So, if the company is seeking to expand internationally, it is a good idea to incorporate a board manager who has already done so; or if it wants to develop its management practices, someone from a more professionalized firm; or if the aim is to diversify, someone familiar with the sectors, technologies or products that the company wants to move into; or if imminent challenges require using high leverage, going public or performing takeovers, someone with experience in these matters.

Directors should have personal and professional qualities enabling them to express opinions and make decisions, even if this jeopardizes their position on the board. To put it plainly, directors cannot be 'yes' men.

Boards of Directors made up entirely of family members are to be found in simple companies; as they gain complexity, they tend to incorporate first members of the firm and then independent directors.

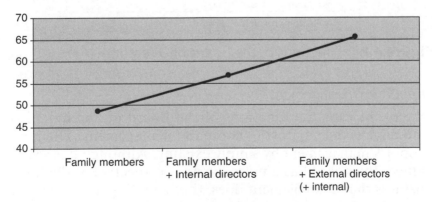

Source: Authors' compilation, FBK Database 2007

Figure A.7 Relationship between business complexity and composition of the Board of Directors

Nevertheless, company executives should be incorporated sparingly into the Board of Directors, because when an executive is acting as a director he or she is above the general manager, and this could easily short-circuit the line of command. Furthermore, there is nothing to prevent senior executives from attending meetings periodically to inform the board about some matter in particular.

Figure A.7 shows that as business complexity grows the origin of the directors gradually broadens, incorporating first inside members and then outside ones.

The Board of Directors of a family business has features that are common to other types of business based on other types of capital, but it also has some specific characteristics.

Functions of the Board of Directors

The Board of Directors in the family business has five main functions, as shown in Figure A.8.

```
● Support for management
● Control over management
● Development of resources and capabilities
● Management succession
● Restrictions on the family
```

Figure A.8   Functions of the Board of Directors

Support for management

One of the essential functions of the Board of Directors is to lend advice and support to company management. The board supports management by simply existing. Although it is seldom valued, the board has a more distant perspective of the family business than management does, thus enabling it to take stock of aspects that management has trouble discerning.

The aphorism about not being able to see the wood for the trees is totally applicable in this case. Because of their involvement in management matters, managers tend to see the trees and have more difficulty making out the wood. The Board of Directors, on the other hand, remains at more of a distance from day-to-day affairs and so is able to see the wood much more easily. Good management requires the ability to see both the trees and the wood.

The board should be made up of individuals with high personal and professional standards. It is very expensive to have incompetent directors. The board must assist the director in aspects such as defining strategies, developing the senior management team, evaluating projects and controlling risks. It is responsible for ensuring that decisions are not only technically correct but also made at the right moment. To this end, it is often better to see the wood than the trees.

The board will be able to provide assistance insofar as it has enough quality information about what is happening in the company. Here the attitude of the top executive is crucial. If the top executive accepts, values and encourages the board, the board will be able to provide assistance. However, often the top executive's vision of the board renders it totally superfluous (see Emperor Model, p. 62).

Monitoring of management

The monitoring of management is one of the principal functions of the Board of Directors. Monitoring means ensuring that the management team is suitably competent and manages the company in the direction indicated by the Family Council.

The monitoring function involves reducing what is known as the 'managerial discretion'[4] of the top executive and his or her team. This means that the General Manager is not empowered to make all types of decisions, and has a much narrower field of action. When there is no Board of Directors, the decision-making capacity of the General Manager is much greater, as is his or her accountability.

If the General Manager is the sole proprietor of the family business, his or her managerial discretion may be much greater, as the outcome will affect his or her assets, but not those of any third party. If the General Manager owns only part of the business, as is usually the case in the second and subsequent generations, it is highly inadvisable for the top executive to have all the control and all the responsibility for the management and governance of the business. All the more so if the General Manager is not a family member. In this case the function of control becomes even more important, as the element of family loyalty as a control factor is not present, although naturally the General Manager should show professional loyalty. However, the loyalty derived from family ties is much stronger than that derived from strictly professional ones.

Control, insofar as it implies sharing responsibility, is good not only for the business and the interests of its owners but also for the General Manager.

Controlling and counselling management are variables that to some extent are at loggerheads,[5] as the board will be able to advise the General Manager insofar as he supplies it with information and raises those issues that are really on his mind at board meetings. This information will also be used to control him, and if this happens, less information may be forthcoming from General Management. In this way, boards generate a certain ambivalence, as the more they seek to control management the less they will be able to advise it, and vice versa. As a result, it is important to strike the right balance between counselling and control, giving more weight to one or the other depending on the situation.

The creation of a Board of Directors in the family business is usually associated with strong emphasis on the advisory function, eventually followed by the gradual incorporation of the function of control. In fact, in its early stages, the Board of Directors can focus exclusively on the advisory function, to the extent that it is often called the Advisory Board.

Development of resources and capabilities

The aspect of resources and capabilities has very seldom been mentioned in connection with the Board of Directors, although we regard it as fundamental.

Businesses compete with each other in terms of the resources and capabilities available to them.[6] Thus, for example, a business with a highly competent management team will be able to perform company takeovers, as it will have the capability to manage the companies it takes over.

Gaining insight into successful behavior in businesses means understanding the resource and capability base that makes that behavior possible. In family business, one fundamental resource is very often the actual entrepreneur. In many cases it is this person who enables the business to compete as it is doing, so with his or her decline or absence the business loses its main resource and capability.

A company's resource and capability base is built up slowly, and the effects of its erosion on the family business tend not to be immediate, which makes it more difficult to identify.

One of the functions of the Board of Directors is to ensure that the business develops resources and capabilities, and that they are sustainable over time. This necessarily entails reducing the firm's dependence on the entrepreneur, without this amounting to wasting his or her capabilities.

This means working away from the business being managed as a single-person outfit, or in other words, working towards a decision-making process based not only on the opinions of the entrepreneur but also on professional criteria. Single-person management does not mean – far from it – that the business is badly run, but it does mean that its running depends on the capabilities of one person. The more extraordinary his or her capabilities, the more difficult they will be to replace.

The function of developing resources and capabilities also includes encouraging the development of second-level manage-ment, thus creating a management team that is capable of leading the company forward without the entrepreneur neces-sarily being at its head. Ultimately, caring for the resource and capability base means ensuring the continuity over time of the firm's ability to compete.

Management succession

Ownership succession is the responsibility of the Family Council, but management succession is the responsibility of the Board of Directors.

The succession of the top executive, when there is no Board of Directors, is an 'all-or-nothing' transition. It means a change from having all the power inherent in the position of the top executive to being removed from the dynamic of the business.

This change presents two basic problems. The first is the loss of the resource constituted by the entrepreneur, and the second is that the drastic nature of the change makes it difficult for him or her to accept. Going from running a family business to playing golf full time is an absurd transition, both for the business and for the entrepreneur.

The Board of Directors should ensure that the quality of management in the business is maintained over time. This means handling the different functions of counselling, control and development of resources and capabilities in a way that is flexible over time.

Figure A.9 shows two different types of relationships between the Board of Directors and General Management. The power of each of them is represented by the size of the oval. In type A we have a General Manager with a large amount of power and a board with little power. Here we are talking about a board that is basically advisory. In type B we have a very different relationship, in which the Board of Directors is very powerful (it advises, monitors and develops resources and capabilities) and General Management less so (it manages but does not govern).

Type A is recommended for the early days of the Board of Directors. It contributes value through the very fact that it exists, the perspective it allows, and its advisory capacity. Above all, this should be the case when the top executive is also the founder of

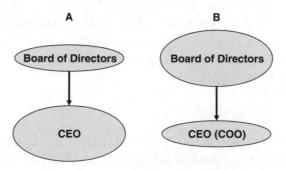

Figure A.9   Management and governance succession

the business. When this is so, taking care of management succession entails the founder standing down from General Management and coming to occupy only the position of Chairman of the Board. This should go hand in hand with a change in the power of each of them, such that the board increases its power (i.e., reinforces its functions of control and development of resources and capabilities) and General Management is left with more operational functions (i.e., less power).

In the case of continuity in second or third generations, the process will be easier and will require less plasticity in the Board of Directors. If the other functions of the board are properly fulfilled, the function of succession will be easier to perform.

Restrictions on the family

It is also the function of the Board of Directors to place restrictions on the intervention of the family in the firm when family criteria take priority over business logic. This is not to say that family members should not be in the Board of Directors, but that theirs is a governance position and not a family one. Therefore, those family members that belong to the Board of Directors must be there on the strength of their competence as board members.[7]

Board members should represent the whole of the Family Council, not just certain members, branches or groups of owners. The logical differences between them should be dealt with in the Family Council, so that there is a single mandate towards the Board of Directors. The board exists to fulfil the mandate of the Family Council. Hence the Board of Directors can be more competent and can create more value for the firm than the boards of other types of companies in which, in contrast, they represent the interests of the shareholders. In such cases the priority of corporate governance takes second place to the defence of private interests. In this type of board, typical of listed companies with a dispersed shareholding, the effort spent on negotiating shareholders' interests may hinder governance capacity.

The Board of Directors should represent the entirety of the owner family. To this end it is important for the Family Council to legitimize the Board of Directors to deal with those aspects that have to do with the family members' professional activity in the business. This means, in other words, everything to do with family members coming to work in the business, their remuneration, their promotion, and if necessary their dismissal. The Board of Directors must also be legitimized by the Family Council to monitor General Management. A highly functional Board of Directors should be in a position to replace the General Manager if necessary.

Summary of the functions of the Board of Directors

Defining the functions of the Board of Directors enables us to assess to what extent it is performing its functions. As we explained in the text, it is not necessary – or even advisable – for all family businesses to have a highly functional Board of Directors; it should be as functional as their needs dictate.

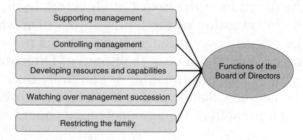

Figure A.10   Functions of the Board of Directors

Executive Committee effectiveness

The Executive Committee is the body responsible for the firm's management decisions. It has three main levels of functioning, depending on the use and the content given to it by the General Manager.

Types of Executive Committee

The three types of committee, in terms of their level of functioning, are:

- Informative committee
- Deliberative committee
- Decision-making committee

Figure A.11   Types of Executive Committee

These three levels are consecutive; thus, a deliberative committee is also informative, and a decision-making committee includes both of the other two functions.

Informative Executive Committee

An informative Executive Committee is one that is used by the General Manager to improve the coordination of activities and the implementation of decisions. In this type of committee, the General Manager maintains a higher hierarchical rank over his or her management team at all times.

The committee is a place for sharing information, in order for members to be better informed and understand the decisions taken by the General Manager. In this way, managers gain a better understanding of their role within the overall dynamics of the company and a broader perspective than is afforded by the information that corresponds to their particular management area.

The dynamics of this type of committee depend on the issues raised by the General Manager, which are usually concerned with the monitoring of operations, evaluation of operational malfunctions, and putting decisions and plans on the table for discussion. It also serves to share any deviations or difficulties that might arise.

The fact that the General Manager performs this coordination task collectively rather than individually with each manager has a positive impact on the dynamics of the group thus created, as it acts as a stimulus for the achievement of objectives. It also helps executives to make the transition from unit management to a broader managerial outlook. This can pave the way for a future evolution towards a deliberative Executive Committee, if the General Manager so wishes.

Deliberative Executive Committee

This Executive Committee acts as a body for analyzing situations from a plural perspective. Although the General Manager sets the standards and the timing and makes the decisions, the committee not only shares information but also discusses possible courses of action and recommends decisions. The ultimate decision, however, lies with the General Manager.

The proper functioning of this type of committee implies freedom of criteria for its members. That is, each member has the right to differ from both the General Manager and the other committee members.

This type of Executive Committee requires higher professional standards than the informative committee. Managers should have the ability to conceive the business as a whole from the position of General Management.

This type of committee improves the quality of decisions and their implementation. Furthermore, decisions are based on more in-depth information and broader knowledge. At the same time there is a greater probability of the management team sharing the diagnosis that justifies the General Manager's decision; this makes for an easier acceptance of the decision and therefore its smoother implementation.

A deliberative committee allows ample development of the management team, as it provides training inasmuch as its members act as virtual general managers. It also fosters their relational skills, as each member treats the other members and the General Manager as equals, only to return to the hierarchical system when they leave the meeting room.

Decision-making Executive Committee

In this case, the main function of the committee is to make the company's high-level operational decisions. We are therefore talking about collective decision-making. Here the big management decisions are made by the Executive Committee as opposed to the General Manager in isolation. This does not mean that everyone involved is on an equal footing, or that the committee can make decisions that are not accepted by the General Manager, but it does mean that decisions are made by consensus. Only in very exceptional situations will the General Manager make a decision that has not previously been accepted by the Executive Committee.

Thus, the Executive Committee is the highest managerial body in the company, even though it is the General Manager who assumes the consequences of this institutionalized management. The General Manager develops the committee because he or she is confident on the quality of the decision made by a group to which he or she belongs.

This decision-making Executive Committee implies a high level of trust by the General Manager in his or her management team, and therefore a high level of trustworthiness among the managers, both professionally and personally.

This type of committee is highly demanding of the General Manager, requiring strong leadership ability. He or she will have little opportunity to resort to authority and 'laying down the law'. High levels of transparency are necessary in the organization, which is not always easy in family business. Suffice to say that there are still organizations that impose restrictions on the management team having access to the company's results and its financial statements.[8]

It also requires high professional standards as regards to members' know-how, relational skills, commitment and self-exigency. A decision-making Executive Committee is the best training ground for future General managers.

Work differentiation

The business and the family are two different systems of a different nature, in which the same people play different roles. In family business it is common to find intermingling and confusion of rules and roles between the two systems.

Business/family differentiation can be clearly seen in aspects such as criteria for access to managerial positions, existing hierarchies and criteria for the remuneration and promotion of family members in executive posts.

Work differentiation refers to the extent to which those family members who are actively involved in the management of the business are so because they belong to the family or because of their professional ability. The greater the presence of family criteria in decisions affecting the working life of the family in the business, the poorer the differentiation will be.

In the introduction we presented the business and the family as two systems that have different functions. The function of the family is to protect, whereas the function of the business is to create value. Offering jobs – especially managerial posts – would appear to be a good way of protecting the family. Company management makes it possible to 'protect' family members by offering them remuneration and social status; being 'such-and-such manager' carries social weight. This, together with the family's tendency towards equality, causes the family to tend to 'invade' managerial positions.

One of the most influential economic theories at present (agency theory)[9] would say that it is good for owners and managers to be the same individuals, as it avoids managers working for their own interests rather than that of the owners, whose interests they are supposed to defend.

In this approach it is assumed that managers occupy managerial positions on the strength of their management capability. However, when they do so in application of family criteria, the result is the weakening of the firm.

Figure A.12 shows how Spanish family businesses have a strong tendency to keep management jobs exclusively in the hands of family members, fix the salaries of family members who work in the firm according to family criteria, and to fix family members' salaries according to criteria of family equality. As examples of this last factor, members of the same generation are often paid the same, and when one family member receives a salary increase, in one way or another the salary of the whole generation ends up improving.

Indicators	Yes
Access to senior management is equal for family members and non-family professionals.	50%
Criteria for setting salaries are the same for family and non-family.	53%
Family members in the same generation have the same salary.[1]	52%
Rules (written or unwritten) govern the setting of family members' salaries.	28%

1. When there are several family members working in the company.

Source: FBK Database, 2007

Figure A.12   Indicators of Work differentiation

Figure A.12 presents some indicators of the degree of Work differentiation existing in Spanish family firms.

Increasing the differentiation between the family and the business entails introducing two basic criteria: first, to select from among the family members the right skill profile to meet the needs of the business; and second, to break the tendency towards family equality.

It is often recommended, and is sometimes even committed to writing in some family constitutions, that the most valid, the most competent family member should join the firm. This is the wrong way to go about building Work differentiation. An approach in terms of who is 'most valid' implies that the rest are 'less valid'. This sort of approach is ultimately perceived by the members of the family not so much as a matter of degree (some professional profiles fit into the business better than others) but rather a matter of some being 'valid' and others 'invalid'.

In the end a dichotomous mentality takes over this approach. Entrepreneurs often ask us to help them find out whether their son or daughter is 'valid' or not. The important thing to realize is that people cannot be divided into the 'valid' and the 'invalid'; everyone has a competencies profile. The decisions as to whether family members should join the firm or not, and if they do, their salary level and opportunities for future promotion, depend on how well their competencies profile meets the firm's needs.

Breaking the criterion of family equality[10] is another of the issues that the family must face in order to develop work differentiation. This is no easy matter, as it is a deeply rooted tendency in the dynamic of the family. To achieve this end, the family must accept that family members – siblings, for example – may relate to one another as equals in some aspects, but do not have to be equal in all.

Each person has his or her own particular skill profile. Breaking equality means being capable of recognizing that one's own profile is different from that of one's sibling. This recognition is what enables us to talk about each person's proper place. For this, it is important to avoid approaches of a competitive nature (who the best sibling is) and instead establish who is best suited for a particular job.

The process of differentiation between the family and the business in the workplace comprises three steps:

a) Define the desired degree of family/business differentiation.
   In other words, to what extent the family wishes to orient itself towards highly selective and demanding access to the business, or else towards greater family protection. The family's capacity to be more protective of itself or less so will depend on the family and business complexity. The greater the complexity, the greater the need for work differentiation.

b) Define the competencies profile required by the business. This is not a simple task, as it requires reflecting on what challenges will need to be faced in the future and how time is going to affect the skills of the present managers. This process can only be successful if we are aware of the fact that in the next generation the company will need different skill profiles from that of the entrepreneur who is currently in charge. It is essential to overcome the tendency to think that in the future the business will need someone who resembles the present leader as closely as possible.

c) Define how this competencies profile is to be assessed. This is another important aspect, as we are dealing with very subjective matters. The assessment each of us makes of ourselves depends to a large extent on our level of self-esteem (some people tend to underestimate themselves and others tend to do the opposite). Those around us also tend to have very biased opinions. Our parents and spouses tend to have highly positive opinions of us, for obvious reasons.

If we are interested in obtaining thorough skill profile assessments we can resort to expert professionals who perform this task following standard processes known in the specialist jargon as assessment centres.[11]

Again, who carries out the assessment and how they do so is no minor consideration. Parents find it difficult to assess their children, and more difficult still to state their assessment explicitly. Parents may pay a very high price, in terms of their relationship with their children, for choosing one over the others.

For this reason it is better if these assessment and decision-making processes are performed at an institutional level. Ideally, the Family Council should define the desired level of differentiation and the Board of Directors should be in charge of defining the required skill profile, making the assessment and choosing between the family members.

Ownership recognition

Family ownership is what makes the family business what it is. A business is a family business because the owners share family ties.

Ownership is so often identified with management in the family firm that the role – and therefore the rights – of the shareholders may not always be recognized. This tends to carry with it insufficient information, difficulty in participating in decisions that affect their ownership strategy, and lack of recognition of their economic rights.

The right of ownership would appear to be obvious in any type of business, but in the case of family businesses it is not so obvious. Clearly, the owners of a business are recognized by law as possessing this right, but here we are not concerned with a legal right but rather the extent to which this right is recognized within the family group.

The family business is built on hard work and good management, not ownership. An entrepreneur or a group of entrepreneurs has an idea, identifies an opportunity and 'goes for it'. The business grows and develops thanks to the effort, the commitment and the capacity to take risks of its founders, and to the teams they have been able to create. The result of this success is a company that has a certain economic value.

While the first generation is in charge of the business, ownership usually carries no rights of its own. Ownership and management are usually seen as the same thing, and so ownership effectively 'does not exist'. The entrepreneur has authority not because he holds all or part of the shares in his company but because he is its founder and the leader who everyone follows.

When younger generations arrive on the scene, the family has to decide what role it wants ownership to play. Giving space to ownership is a slow process, and not always an easy one. Thus, for example, in a great many family businesses, a request for information from a family member who does not work in the company is seen as lack of trust, and asking for a dividend is seen as a lack of commitment to the family business.

Recognition of ownership is associated with something that is taken for granted in other types of structures, namely the subordination of management to ownership. Anything less means that the managers decide what information they give to the owners, and what dividends they pay out to them.

Low recognition of ownership means that the company is the 'domain' of the managers, who share power with the owners if and when they see fit. If we take this situation to an extreme, we may find a very comfortable situation in which managers run a company without the need to generate a return for the owners.

Poor recognition of shareholders' rights constitutes an incentive to work in the family business, as this is the only way to form part of the firm and obtain income, status and information. This often leads to inoperative situations such as working in the family business 'to represent my branch of the family' or limits along the lines of 'one person working per family branch'.

Work differentiation and recognition of ownership should go hand in hand.[12] When a family incorporates business criteria in order to enable family members to join the firm professionally, it has to restrict the power of the managers in order to grant space to the owners. Insofar as the right to obtain a dividend is recognized, it will also be easier to remunerate management on a performance basis.

One aspect that we will not dwell on here but that we would nevertheless like to mention is that the family should state what sort of ownership they are bringing to bear: legal ownership (recognition of the ownership rights of the holders of shares or stock) or psychological ownership (recognition of the ownership rights of those who act as owners, regardless of whether they may not yet be so legally because they have not received the inheritance, or whether they may no longer be the legal owners because of a transfer inter vivos).

Low levels of legitimation of ownership also tend to be associated with confusion between these two types of ownership. Thus, ownership may be in the hands of a senior generation but the ownership rights may be exercised by their children, or vice versa. Non-coincidence between psychological ownership and legal ownership makes recognition of ownership more difficult.

Family accountability

The founding entrepreneur of a company has highly self-demanding standards; otherwise he or she would not be an entrepreneur.

As family and business complexity grows, a self-demanding attitude is not enough. Greater family complexity signals greater diversity between family members' standards about their own behavior, and ultimately leads to problems in the family and the business.

The most self-demanding family member of those who work in the firm becomes fed up with being the one who 'does all the donkey work', while those who are less self-demanding 'take advantage' of the situation. Equally, as the business becomes more complex, higher standards should be demanded of management.

As a result, it is essential for the family business to incorporate external exigency. Although it is very important to be self-demanding, it is not enough. Managers must be held accountable depending on the position they hold. This exigency should come from their hierarchical superior, whether this is an individual or a governance body.

However, in a family business, a professional (whether a family member or not) can only be demanding with a family professional if he or she is legitimized by the family. The same can be said about governance bodies. A Board of Directors can only be demanding with a family executive if it is legitimized to do so by the family. Hence family accountability is an important dimension for a proper structuring of the family/business relationship.

A good way of introducing this concept is with an example. An entrepreneur might invite his son to come and work in the firm, and put him under the orders of an executive he trusts, with the following mandate: 'Push him as if he weren't my son, just like any other employee.' We wonder how far this executive will be able to push 'the owner's son'. There will be times when the executive will indeed be able to push him just like any other employee, and there will be other times when doing so will amount to an act of heroism.

The whereabouts of the threshold beyond which this junior family member cannot be pushed will depend on the level of Family accountability developed by the family, i.e., to what extent the family is demanding when playing ownership roles, but also requires its members to be accountable when occupying management roles.

In the example above, only if the family legitimizes the executive to hold the young recruit responsible can he do so in such a way that it is actually recognized as being in fulfilment of his obligations. If family accountability is lacking, any attempt to be demanding with 'the owner's son' is likely to lead to problems for the executive. He will therefore have to choose between, on the one hand, being genuinely demanding with the family member and possibly jeopardizing his career and, on the other, accommodating himself to the situation and simulating exigency.

These dynamics are non-explicit, and furthermore denied; a family with low family accountability is unlikely to admit that this is the case.[13] Nevertheless, non-family professionals have a keen sensitivity for knowing how far they are legitimized to be professionally exigent with family members and how far these members are 'protected' by their family aura. A high family accountability enables family members to develop as professionals in their family business.

Family accountability also affects the highest levels of the business. Figures A.13, A.14 and A.15 reflect only three of the indicators that tell us that the standards of Family accountability to be found in Spanish family businesses are quite low. We could say that the Spanish family business rests on high standards of self-exigency but very low levels of external exigency.

Figure A.13 shows that in 68% of cases the family and the Board of Directors have never had a formal discussion about the performance of the General Manager; his performance has never been assessed. And a family business that cannot assess its General Manager is a business in risk. As long as he is competent and

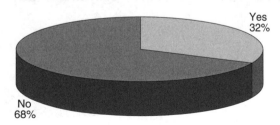

Source: FBK Database, 2007

Figure A.13 Have you assessed the General Manager's performance?

remains so throughout the period he holds the position, the company will function, but if his level of competence slips, the family business has no mechanism with which to demand results.

The ultimate proof of Family accountability, the 'quick ratio', so to speak, is whether a family business can replace a General Manager who is a family member if results are consistently bad. This will only be possible, without causing a serious crisis, if Family accountability is very well developed.

As can be seen in Figure A.14, the ability to replace the General Manager with a consistently bad performance is very low.

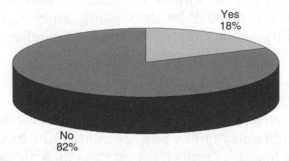

Source: FBK Database, 2007

Figure A.14   Would the General Manager be replaced if results were consistently bad?

The same happens with the Board of Directors. Figure A.15 shows that in 63% of cases there has been no formal discussion,[14] either inside or outside the board, regarding its performance.

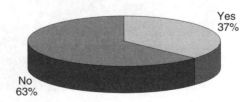

Source: FBK Database, 2007

Figure A.15   Have you assessed the performance of the Board of Directors?

Developing Family accountability involves working with soft elements of structure. For a family to develop high levels of Family accountability, it must develop a family culture of effort and commitment, together with a certain distance between the family and the business. In Chapter 3 we explained why this can only happen in some family business models and not in others.

Professionalism of management practices

The concept of professionalization is less obvious than it might seem at first sight. Because of this, we will start by explaining what, for us, professionalization is not.

In the context of family business, the term 'professionalization' has usually been understood as the process of incorporating senior executives from outside the family into the family business. This is not professionalization as we understand it in our management model. In the above section on family/business differentiation we discussed how the roles and rules of each system should be separated so that managerial positions are not made available for the mere fact of belonging to the family. By the same logic, no one is any less professional for the mere fact of belonging to the family.

Professionalizing a company has nothing to do with the origin of the people who run it. Rather, it is a discipline and a form of management that deals with different aspects of content (what professional managers do with the tools they use and their contingency), i.e., with the aspects that affect their decision. This is how management has come to be defined as a discipline.[15]

A family business seeking to develop the professionalism of its management practices should work in two directions: to create deliberate strategies and to build decentralized structures.

Deliberate strategies

Entrepreneurial (non-professionalized) management tends towards emergent strategies,[16] i.e., strategies that the entrepreneur has in his head and does not necessarily share with his management team. Often he would be unable to share them even if he wanted to, as they are intuitive. The entrepreneur's in-depth knowledge of his sector and his business enables him to see clearly what needs to be done and to take advantage of opportunities as they arise without 'going astray'. This may be a great way of defining strategies, but it restricts the evolution of the business to the capabilities of the entrepreneur and his life cycle.

Creating deliberate strategies involves verbalizing strategy. It means that senior management must define and communicate clearly the strategy of the company. This will allow the various members of the management team to independently make decisions that are aligned with the explicitly stated strategy. Confident decision-making is not possible unless one knows where the company is heading.

If strategy is not deliberate, managers cannot be competent in their decision-making, and so become mere executors of the entrepreneur's decisions. When the time of his or her decline or absence arrives, the organization lacks the capacity to make decisions because it is made up of individuals and practices that may be very efficient when it comes to executing but have no decision-making ability.

The argument usually wielded by the entrepreneur for not evolving in this direction is that deliberate strategy involves missing opportunities. This should not be the case, since deliberate does not mean rigid. Deliberate strategy actually makes it possible to take greater advantage of opportunities, as it widens the group of people who are capable of identifying when changes mean opportunities for the business.

Decentralized structures

Professionalization entails building decentralized structures. Entrepreneurial management is characterized by centralizing decision-making around the figure of the entrepreneur. He is the only person who knows what to do, so decisions go through him. By making the decisions, he is able to keep control over the organization. The entrepreneur knows what needs to be done at any given moment, because he gives the word. As a result, he needs to equip the firm with a good structure with the ability to execute.

By decentralizing its structure, the organization is able to make, implement and control the most appropriate decisions and ensure that they are all properly aligned. Building decentralized structures is a slow task with multiple dimensions, including the skill profile of the management team, leadership style, decision-making processes, coordination systems, incentive systems, control systems, information flows, commitment management, etc.

The more professionalized a company's management practices, the greater its stability.

Information structuring

As we mentioned earlier when discussing knowledge, professionalization is related to the generation of 'explicit knowledge', as opposed to tacit knowledge.[17] Explicit knowledge is knowledge that can be transmitted to others in an ordered fashion.

A good footballer may know how to take a free kick, but he is unable to explain it. In other words, he has tacit knowledge, but he cannot express it. This is the case with many experts, and not only in artistic or subjective disciplines, but also in other more analytical ones. Tacit knowledge is to be found in music, in looking for wild mushrooms, in prospecting for water or for oil, in medicine and in scientific research. And this can undoubtedly be applied to business.

An expert entrepreneur knows a great deal, thanks to his background and experience, but he does not always know how to share it. He often has difficulty in explaining 'how to take a free kick'. In this way, the whole weight of the organization falls back onto his shoulders.

Developing management practices requires stating knowledge explicitly, so that it can easily be shared within the organization and enabling new arrivals in the organization to benefit from it. This means formalizing processes (e.g., ISO standards), creating databases with information about the organization's range of activities (e.g., SAP) and developing systems of indicators and management control (scorecards, reporting systems, etc.).

Professionalization of management practices and structuring of information are two activities that are closely related, as they depend on each other and are developed jointly.[18]

The transition from an organization with entrepreneurial management to one with a highly developed management provides the business with greater stability, by making it less dependent on the talent of one single person and allowing it to take advantage of the talent of a whole team of people.

If this transition is done properly, the business does not have to lose the virtues of an entrepreneurial organization, and at the same time will incorporate the stability of professionalized management.

Figure A.16 summarizes the characteristics of entrepreneurial management on the one hand and professionalized organization on the other.

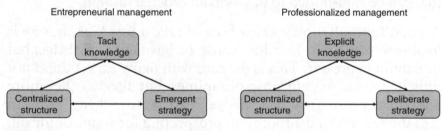

Figure A.16 Entrepreneurial management versus professionalized management

Differences management

For an appropriate handling of differences it is necessary to gain insight into communication and its characteristics.

Any process of human communication will have three characteristics:

a) It happens between at least two people.
b) Those involved use words or body language.
c) It takes place in a particular context.

The context in which the communication takes place provides its meaning. Information has a value that depends on the place, the specific situation and the relationship between those engaged in the communication. The phrase 'hands up!' is an order. But its meaning and the behavior it generates are very different if the person receiving the order is walking down a dark alley or in the middle of a gymnastics class.

We are all experts at recognizing these spaces and adjusting our conduct accordingly. We all behave differently depending on whether we are in an office, in a church, at a football ground or at home. We are used to switching effortlessly from one context to another, adopting the appropriate behavior for each particular place. All communication has a meaning that depends on the context in which it takes place. A joke by a workmate might be taken well enough at a party, but the same comment might be taken very badly in a meeting at work.

Everyone plays different roles in different contexts, whether the family or the business, depending on the place they occupy and the function they are assigned. One can act as father, mother, son, daughter, grandson, nephew or whatever in the family, and at the same time shareholder, departmental manager, general manager or chairman of the board in the business. This means different roles with different functions, played by the same people.

In a family business it is easy to imagine the risk involved in slipping between two so close yet so different contexts as family and work. The idea defended by some, whereby all the siblings are entitled to a similar job in the family business and the same salary, is nothing but a case of family rules slipping from the family context (where all siblings are equal) into the business context, where the rules are different.

The effort required of the members of a business family is far greater than that required of a non-business family. Their double membership (of the family and the business) requires the ability to relate simultaneously in different contexts (this is an office and the rules are those of the workplace; now we're at home, under family rules, and we'll behave as parents and children, or siblings).

In order to find creative solutions to this difficulty it is important to communicate about communication (metacommunicate), that is, come to an agreement about where, how and when to use one or another set of rules. The development of the capacity to meta-communicate is a necessary condition for a family to be able to successfully combine life at home and in a shared workplace.

All communication involves two aspects that occur simultaneously: content and relationship. Content is about the issues that are discussed, whereas relationship has to do with the position of one speaker with respect to the other. For example, the way a student expresses himself when talking to a classmate about his disagreement with the mark he has been given for an exam is not the same as the dialogue this same student has with the teacher when he asks for his exam to be re-marked.

Two types of communicative relationships can occur between two people or groups of people, independently of content. Relationships can be 'up-down' (complementary) or 'across'(symmetric).[19]

'Up-down' relationships are those in which one person is in a position of superiority over the other, who is in a position of inferiority. It is the case of teacher-pupil, boss-employee, father-son, expert-apprentice, protector-protected, coach-player, dominator-dominated and many other such relationships.

'Across' relationships are those in which the two people relate on an equal footing. Examples would be relationships between workmates, friends, members of a team, siblings and so on.

The traditional model of the couple used to be an 'up-down' relationship (with the man dominating the woman), but 'across' relationships have been the norm for couples for some time now (neither feels that he or she has the right to be in a position of superiority over the other).

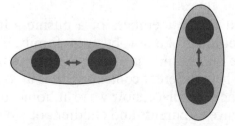

Figure A.17   'Up-down' versus 'across' relationships

Differences management in the family business involves the family learning not to have rigid relationships. Parents, for example, should not always be in a position of superiority over their children, and siblings or cousins do not always have to relate to one another as equals. In other words, they have to learn that in the business context they may have an 'up-down' relationship if one of them is higher up in the organization chart.

The Board of Directors and the Family Council will work better with relationships of equality, that is, if no one considers himself to be superior or inferior, but rather as a member with equal rights.

When siblings have the opportunity to relate on an 'up-down' basis, they can take advantage of the differences that exist between them. The best of each sibling is not what makes them the same (the fact of being siblings) but what makes them different, namely his or her skill profile. The rivalry created by equality is a hindrance to taking advantage of the best they have to offer.

When we talk of differences we mean more than just the roles family members play in the business and the hierarchical levels they occupy. We are also talking about their personal profiles and the dominant interests as regards the meaning the business holds for each family member.

In our account of family complexity (Chapter 2), we referred to the variety of dominant interests that tends to exist in a large family group. Thus, the family firm will mean, for some members, job security; for others, an opportunity to develop his or her entrepreneurial leanings; and for still others, a potential for activating his or her investment in economic results. All legitimate interests, but oriented towards goals that do not always coincide.

When these interests are not clearly defined, conversation may prove to be a source of misunderstandings.

Imagine a conversation between two brothers or cousins about an investment. For one of them, with interests oriented towards growth, the investment is fundamental, and he has reasons to defend its advisability. But if the other has more conservative interests, whether it is to keep his job or to maintain a particular level of dividends, he might see the investment as a risk to stability, and consequently adduce reasons against the project. The risk lies not in the existence of differences, but in the fact of not taking these differences into account. If each knows the position of the other with regard to his interests he will find the way to accommodate them. However, if these differences are not explicit they will not be taken into consideration in the conversation, and each will try to convince the other on the basis of his own reasons.

When communicating about the family business, awareness of differences of interests and positions between each of the members taking part is a determining factor. Otherwise conversations will not be opportunities to build agreements and establish relationships of trust, but the opposite: arguing, annoyance and mistrust.

Families who understand and handle their differences well succeed in maintaining clear and free-flowing communication in aspects concerning the family business, and create a climate of trust among their members; trust that enables them to talk openly about disagreements, find solutions together and so reach agreements.

Explicitation of rules

All social behavior is governed by implicit or explicit rules, and therefore so is the family business. The rules of a social system are behavioral guidelines and limits for its members as a whole. They are not the same as a regulation, in the sense of an explicit statement of a limit that must be respected. Thus, in Spain the regulation as regards the speed limit on motorways is 120 kph, while the general trend is that people seldom drive slower than this, and cars often go at 130 or 140 kph without society as a whole feeling that a rule is being broken.

Just like any other social system, the family business is governed by countless rules, most of them implicit. Rules define the distribution of power, access to jobs, distribution of economic flows and rights, communication patterns, approaches to succession and so on.

The greatest difficulty in creating rules that work in each specific case lies in their explicit statement. If a family is capable of making explicit its main rules governing its relationship with the business, it will be capable of altering them to maintain their level of functional usefulness at any given time.

In family business it is important to be able to change the rules in order to adapt them to increasing complexity. Rules change either as a result of agreement between people or as a result of a crisis. Logically, agreement is recommendable. And for this to happen, it is necessary to be able to talk about the rules.

In a great many family firms, there are rules that cannot be made explicit because they are 'unsightly'; those involved are not prepared to admit that they exist. Rules such as 'things are done the way the founder wants them to be done,' 'the heirs do whatever they like' or 'nobody can demand anything of a family member' are unlikely to be admitted by a family. Nevertheless, a non-family member of the company or an outside observer can see that these are the rules that are practised in that company.

Families that practice these sorts of rules usually verbalize socially desirable rules; for example that the family participates, that the heirs are professionals and that everyone has a right to express his or her opinion.

When drawing up a family constitution, the important thing is not to fix socially desirable rules, as happens all too often, but to explicitly state the rules that are actually practised, and to come to an agreement as to how they might be suitably modified to take account of the new levels of complexity, or future levels. Under these circumstances, a family constitution is a useful tool for the explicit statement of rules.

Entrepreneurial capability

Businesses do not develop just because they have highly institutionalized governance structures or professionalized management practices. The development of a company also requires vitality, eagerness to do things, the ability to undertake ventures.

To start up a business is to develop an entrepreneurial project. The innovation generated by technology and the competitive dynamic makes the period that an entrepreneurial project remains relevant shorter and shorter.

One generation's project is unlikely to be viable during the next generation. A generation cannot, therefore, maintain the competitiveness of its family business by continuing the project of the previous generation. In other words, by doing the same but better. This approach leads to a gradual erosion of the family firm's ability to compete. If the company is robust this process is usually slow, so the family can easily be unaware of it.

It is usual in a succession process to focus on the aspects of planning and distribution of ownership. These aspects demand so much attention that it is common to lose sight of the importance of ensuring that entrepreneurship is the pivot on which succession turns.

Entrepreneurship can manifest itself through the ability to generate a strategic renewal of the family group, but also through the ability to generate new ventures within the group.

Some studies of entrepreneurial businesses show that they share certain fundamental characteristics,[20] which should be retained or even increased, if possible, with the generational transition.

Proactivity

This refers to the ability to detect and take advantage of new opportunities. In times of great changes in technologies, markets and habits, a host of new opportunities arise. Very often, consolidated family businesses fail to take advantage of these new opportunities, given the difficulty involved in identifying them, the perceived risks or the barriers encountered against the necessary internal change.

Opportunities are increasingly distant from the world in which consolidated companies move. In companies with a high technological content, opportunities are more often explored by younger people with the capacity to generate initiatives and create disruptions. The success of companies led by very young people (Google, Skype, MySpace, etc.) is frequently put down to the enormous capability of these young entrepreneurs.

Although it is true that these are extremely capable young people, their initiatives emanate from the huge quantity of entrepreneurial initiatives that are generated in all sectors throughout the globe. It is undoubtedly true that the merit of an outstanding footballer is of his own making, but it is also due to the existence of thousands of youths playing and training hard, striving to be great. Out of quantity comes forth quality.

A family business cannot take this sort of approach, as the option of quantity is not open to it. In the family there will be one entrepreneur – or more than one, with luck; but no large number that might enable quantity to come up with quality. This is where complexity becomes an advantage.

Having aspirations that go beyond the possible does not mean being reckless. Aspiration stretches the organization, and in the long run makes possible that which seemed impossible. It is not the same as being unrealistic. Entrepreneurial businesses are very realistic at each step they take, but at the same time highly ambitious when it comes to defining the direction and the vision of their organization.

Teamwork

Teamwork is another feature of entrepreneurial businesses. Entrepreneurial businesses are built on the vitality, creativity and commitment of the various groups of people. In family businesses, initially it is the founder who provides these qualities. This should not prevent these entrepreneurs from being capable of creating a team to follow them and carry the projects through. All founders surround themselves with a team of 'right-hand men', a *troupe de corps* of staunch supporters. These staunch supporters are not necessarily great professionals when taken individually, but they nevertheless form a team that, together with the founder, is capable of doing great things.

The next generation has to keep up this teamwork, but changing the way the team holds together, and probably also the identity of its members. Next generations must often face the practical and ethical problem of how to renew the entrepreneurial team and at the same time be loyal and recognize the work it has done.

The transition of the entrepreneurial team from the first to the second generation should incorporate this qualitative change from a team that focuses on a strong leader to one that focuses on a common project. If the second generation has succeeded in making this change, the following generations will be simpler as regards this dimension.

Capacity for solving dilemmas

The development of 'the new' brings the family business face to face with contradictory situations: how to innovate yet preserve what has been achieved so far; how to be respectful to a parent yet at the same time assume power over the running of the business; how to treat one's sons and daughters equally yet at the same time empower the most enterprising of them.

Having entrepreneurship means having developed the skill to move in this world of dilemmas. It means abandoning the absolute, abandoning dichotomous thinking. There are not just two possibilities: black and white, useful and useless, good and evil.

Entrepreneurial families approach reality through the range of greys.[21] This enables them to take pragmatic and moderate courses of action, seeking out the most appropriate ways forward in each situation and circumstance. This approach is contrary to that of 'excellence', where there is a superior way of doing things and that is how they should be done. This is absolute thinking, and it is not a practice that family businesses are used to.

Capacity for learning

Entrepreneurial family businesses have a great capacity for learning. This capacity is consubstantial with entrepreneurs, who have been able to transmit it to their organization. In these enterprises, it is not just the entrepreneur who learns but the whole organization.

Learning involves the ability to change and innovate. Family businesses often lose their learning capacity once they have got past the first generation. When the family firm focuses its learning capacity on the entrepreneur rather than the organization, innovation remains 'fixed' in the previous generation.

Entrepreneurial behavior requires that learning will not come to a halt during the long period of intergenerational coexistence; the new generations should be able to experience the new by making a contribution on their own.

Non CEO dependence

Family businesses are often unaware that the top executive is a basic resource for the company's competitive ability. To talk of resources (or resources and capabilities, which is the concept used by the resource-based theory)[22] is to talk of those elements that enable the business to successfully develop the competitive strategies it is implementing.

The ability to compete depends on the resources and capabilities that a company develops and is capable of putting to good use. Resources can be tangible (factories, patents, etc.), intangible (brands, trust, etc.), human (capabilities of the members of the company) or organizational (processes, coordination systems, information flows, etc.).

The importance of a resource is clearly perceived when it disappears. Just think of the collapse of Arthur Andersen due to the disappearance of the resource brand-reputation-trust.

In family business the entrepreneur is a fundamental resource for the company's ability to compete. All the more so if it is the founder. As a result, the lesser the dependence of the future of the family business on one single individual, the more stable it will be and the better prepared it will be for succession.

This is not to say that it is not important for the top executive to be a very able person, but it does mean that it is crucial for the company to depend as little as possible on this valuable person.

Developing non-dependence on the top executive[23] is closely linked to the whole range of dimensions of structure that we have dealt with above, especially the creation of an institutional structure, the development of management and the development of entrepreneurship.

Succession planning

So far we have dealt with aspect relating to management succession, and now we will turn our attention to those relating to ownership succession.

Ownership succession must first of all be conceived from the perspective of family complexity. The number of owners and their degrees of kinship determine the family complexity. Therefore, both the generation in power and the next one must be aware that if they decide to increase the family complexity they will have to develop the relationship structures between the family and the business to match the new circumstances.

Ownership succession must take several aspects into account: tax issues, wills, and agreements on asset, corporate and economic matters.

Succession planning can be divided into two main aspects: a strategic one and a legal and administrative one.

The strategic component is concerned with the decision about who is going to hold shares in the company in the next generation. This has a direct impact on family complexity. Although the general trend at present is for all the children to receive an equal proportion of the shares, it is important for the generation in power to address this decision taking into account how it affects family complexity and the structure development that comes with it.

Another fundamental aspect to determine is the future economic relationship between the two generations. Ownership succession should not necessarily be understood as a donation, i.e., as a transaction made without any economic compensation. There is the possibility of reaching a monetary agreement whereby the generation that gives up ownership is guaranteed sufficient income for the future. This issue is particularly relevant in the case of families with small or medium-sized enterprises in which the assets are strongly concentrated in the company.

The legal and administrative component of succession calls for several aspects to be taken into account: tax issues, wills, marriage settlements and corporate matters.

A wide difference exist in Europe in the taxation of the inheritance and gift tax. Each entrepreneur should seek advice from a tax specialist to ensure that these conditions are met.

Although it might seem obvious, it is worth insisting that all owners should have their wills properly drawn, including all agreements reached by the family regarding the transfer of shares. The succession should be accompanied by agreements between the heirs regarding spouses' rights in the event of death or divorce. These agreements should also be reflected in the corresponding stock syndication agreements contained in the articles of association.

Succession planning is also a good opportunity for the family to rethink the corporate structure of its companies. Beyond a certain complexity, it is recommendable to create holding-type structures allowing easier control over the companies in the group.

In any event, succession planning should be carried out by an expert adviser in legal and financial affairs.

NOTES

Chapter 1

1 J. Nieto, *Estructura, estrategia y conocimiento. Una lectura histórica de la política de gestión* (Structure, strategy and knowledge. A historical reading of management policy). Unpublished doctoral thesis. ESADE-URL, 2006.

2 The Thyssen group pioneered management in the 19th century, by introducing vertical integration structures, control systems, multidivisional structure, etc. (J. R. Fear. *August Thyssen and the construction of German corporate management*, Harvard University Press, 2005), although these innovations have traditionally been attributed to American corporations.

3 Wharton School at the University of Pennsylvania.

4 Creator of the Bethlehem Steel Company, once the second largest in the United States.

5 Louis B. Barnes and Simon A. Hershon, 'Transferring power in the family business', *Harvard Business Review*, Boston, vol. 54, No. 4 (July–Aug. 1976), p. 105.

6 L. Danco, *Beyond Survival: A Business Owner's Guide for Success*, The Center for Family Business, Cleveland, 1975, and L. Danco, *Inside the Family Business*, The Center for Family Business, Cleveland, 1983.

7 P. Davis and D. Stern, 'Adaptation, survival, and growth of the family business: an integrated systems perspective', *Human Relations*, vol. 34, No. 4 (1980), pp. 207–224.

8 In advanced societies a host of different social systems coexist (political parties, sports clubs, neighborhood associations, educational centers, religious confessions, colonies of immigrants, professional groups, administrations, families, businesses, etc.). People as individuals belong simultaneously to different social systems without any disorder, as there is no confusion about which system they are in at any given moment. Thus, someone can be the leader of a political party, but when he is at his children's school he belongs to that social system as a parent role, not as a political leader. Therefore, his behavior will be different; it will not occur to him to give orders to the other members, as he would in his party. The problem with interpenetration of systems [see E. Kepner, 'The family and the firm: A co-evolutionary perspective', *Organizational Dynamics*, vol. 12, No. 1 (1983), pp. 57–70] is that they transmit disorder to each other, as it is not clear when a person belongs to one system or the other. So, if there were interpenetration between the political system and the school systems , the political leader might stick posters of his political campaign up in the school playground, and the head

teacher might call the parents of a party member to try to redress his bad behavior. Interpenetration causes confusion and disorder.

9 John Davis is now Chair of Family Business at Harvard University.

10 R. Tagiuri and J. A. Davis, 'Bivalent attributes of the family firm', *Family Business Review*, vol. 9, No. 2 (1996), pp. 199–208. This paper was first published in 1982 as a Harvard Business School working paper.

11 K. E. Gersick, J. A. Davis, M. M. Hampton and I. Lansberg, *Generation to Generation: Life Cycles of the Family Business*, Harvard Business School Press, 1997.

12 This is shown in an empirical study conducted by one of the authors of this book on a sample of family businesses in the region of Madrid (Gimeno, 2005).

13 J. Ward, *Keeping the Family Business Healthy*, San Francisco, Jossey-Bass, 1988.

14 FBK Database, 2007.

15 See the section 'Management in the Emperor Model' (p. 111).

16 H. Morikawa and K. Kobayashi, *Development of Managerial Enterprise*, Tokyo, 1986. The Sumitomo family code dates from 1891, and that of Mitsui from 1900.

17 A. Gimeno and G. Baulenas, 'Contenido y tipos de protocolo en la empresa familiar española', in: Amat, Joan M. and Corona, Juan F. (eds), *El protocolo familiar*, Deusto, Barcelona, 2007.

18 J. Ward, *Keeping the Family Business Healthy*, Jossey-Bass, San Francisco, 1988.

19 J. Ward, *Creating Effective Boards for Private Enterprises: Meeting the Challenges of Continuity and Competition*, Jossey-Bass, San Francisco, 1991.

20 F. Neubauer and A. G. Lank, *The Family Business*, Palgrave Macmillan, 1998.

21 This point will be discussed in the section 'Institutionalization' (p. 45).

22 *Idem.*

23 As an illustrative example, 24% of the boards of directors of Spanish family firms have no knowledge of the accounts of the companies they administer. That is to say that they fulfill the legal formality of administering the firms (and take personal responsibility for it), but they do not have the minimum information that would allow us to suppose that they perform some sort of governance function (FBK Database, 2007).

24 www.ffi.org.

Chapter 2

1 Thus, for example, it is impossible to predict all the ups and downs that a young couple will have to face in forming a family, but it is easy, however,

to anticipate that they will go through an adjustment stage before they can create a common life style; that in view of the fact that the average duration of marriage is 13.8 years (//www.ipfe.org/Informe_Evolucion_Familia_Europa_2006_Espanol.pdf), divorce is a strong possibility; that when they have their first child, if they have one, they will go through a learning period as parents, etc.

2 Chaos theory provides a clear explanation of why this level of prediction is not possible. For further reading we recommend: I. Prigogine (1997), *The End of Certainty*, The Free Press, New York, 1997.

3 We will go into these concepts in greater depth in Chapter 3.

4 On the whole, it is unwise to reduce complexity by means of division among several family members, as it tends to weaken the competitive position of the resulting companies, when there are synergies among them, as is usually the case. These types of options lean towards the phenomenon of the 'business smallholding'.

5 P. Ariès and G. Duby, *A History of Private Life*, Volume V, Belknap Press of Harvard, 1987, pp. 14–19, 23.

6 For further reading on these aspects we recommend the following authors: J. L. Linares, *Identidad y narrativa*, Paidós Terapia Familiar, Barcelona, 1996.
S. Minuchin, *Families and Family Therapy*, Harvard University Press, Cambridge (Massachusetts), 1974.
D. Reiss, *The Family's Construction of Reality*, Harvard University Press, Cambridge (Massachusetts), 1981.

7 Based on I. Lansberg, 'Managing human resources in family firms: the problem of institutional overlap', *Organizational Dynamics,* vol. XII, No. 1 (1983), pp. 39–46.

8 A. Gimeno, G. Labadie, W. Saris and X. Mendoza, 'Internal factors of family business performance: an integrated theoretical model', in P. Poutziouris, K. Smyrnios and S. Klein, *Handbook of Research on Family Business*, Edward Elgar Publishing, 2006, pp. 149–164.

9 G. Lakoff, *Women, Fire and Dangerous Things*, The University of Chicago Press, Chicago, 1987.

10 A combination of the protective and the financial orientation is unlikely, as in the former the business owner is concerned with work and in the latter with having people working for him. Both can obtain income from the business, but the former wants significant income to reach a decent standard of living (the definition of 'decent' being a moot point) and the latter wants the income to be greater than that provided by any other alternative investment (although he is also interested in controlling the risk and obtaining liquidity).

11 We would do well to reflect on who remembers companies like Digital, Woolworth or PanAm today, and the fact that current market leaders like Dell, Wal-Mart or EasyJet hardly existed 30 years ago. The same can be applied to whole industries, as merchant banking.

12 Mexico was an example to the world with Salinas de Gortari (1988–1994) until it fell into the Tequila Crisis. Similarly, Argentina was regarded as an example when it fixed the austral to the US dollar (1985), only to fall into a deep crisis. Iceland is a recent case of shift of one of the richest countries in the world to almost default.

13 Most of the companies identified as 'excellent' in Peters and Waterman's celebrated book *In Search of Excellence* went through serious difficulties in the years following publication.

14 Jeffrey Skilling (Enron), Calisto Tanzi (Parmalat), Lee Jueun (Hyundai) Bernard Madoff (Madoff Investment Securities) and Mario Conde (Banesto) are just some of the 'fallen idols' of recent years.

15 The group is Inditex, but we refer to its best-known brand for ease of recognition.

16 The FBK Database (2007) was generated over the period 2000–2007 by compiling the information supplied anonymously by family businesses in order to run the FBK Diagnostic self-testing tool. The most notable project was *Radiografía de la Empresa Familiar Española* (Spotlight on the Spanish Family Business), conducted in the years 2005–2006 by ESADE and FBK with the collaboration and support of the Family Firm Institute (FFI) and BBVA. The project culminated in a study on 1,237 Spanish family businesses. See www.fbkonline.com/es/eventos/index.html for further reading.

17 We recommend reading the section on structure in the annex (p. 122), where this subject is discussed in greater detail.

18 For further information see the section 'Existence of institutions' in the annex (p. 122).

19 For further information see the section 'Family Council Effectiveness' in the annex (p. 129).

20 For further information see the section 'Board of Directors Effectiveness' in the annex (p. 131).

21 For further information see the section 'Executive Committee Effectiveness' in the annex (p. 140).

22 For further information see the section 'Work differentiation' in the annex (p. 143).

23 For further information see the section 'Ownership recognition' in the annex (p. 147).

24 For further information see the section 'Family accountability' in the annex (p. 149).

25 For further information see the section 'Professionalism of management practices' in the annex (p. 153).

26 For further information see the section 'Information structuring' in the annex (p. 155).

27 For further information see the section 'Differences management' in the annex (p. 156).

28 For further information see the section 'Explicitation of rules' in the annex (p. 160).

29 For further information see the section 'Entrepreneurial capability' in the annex (p. 161).
30 Here we use the negative formulation 'non-dependence' so that a high development of this dimension will imply a high structure development.
31 For further information see the section 'Non Ceo dependence' in the annex (p. 165).
32 For further information see the section 'Succession planning' in the annex (p. 166).

Chapter 3

1 A. Gimeno et al, *Radiografía de la Empresa Familiar Española: Fortalezas y Riesgos*, ESADE, FBK, IEF, BBVA, Barcelona, 2006.
2 The technical term for this type of analysis is cluster analysis.
3 This curve was approximated by calculating the frequency distribution of each family business model as a function of the age of the firm, this being divided into ten-year periods. In this way, the graph shows that approximately 45% of the firms studied that were less than ten years old belonged to the Captain Model. The curve corresponds to the second-order polynomial of the average frequency of the model in question, in this case the Captain Model.
4 Here managerial discretion is understood as the broad decision-making powers of a manager without the need to seek authorization from a higher level. In the case of the Captain and Emperor Models there is no higher level, because of the low degree of institutionalization; the Board of Directors is either non-existent or inoperative. The concept was first proposed by Williamson (O. E. Williamson, *The Economics of Discretionary Behaviour: Managerial Objectives in a Theory of the Firm*, Prentice-Hall, 1964), to refer to managers' ability to address objectives other than making a profit.
5 There are also external factors (sector, position in the value chain, etc.) that also exert an influence, but they are not taken into account in this analysis precisely because they are external. The fact of being a family firm is internal to the firm (it is its ownership structure) and therefore the models likewise only incorporate internal factors.
6 In this section we only compare the five models for which we have quantitative data.
7 This distinction is widely developed in philosophy (epistemology), sociology (constructivism), linguistics and cognitive science. For further reading we recommend: John Dewey (1960) *Experience and Nature and The Quest for Certainty*, G.P. Putnam's Sons Edition.
8 See the section 'Communication' (p. 52) for further discussion of the meaning of 'conducting relationships from above'.
9 History is full of the failures of emperors who did not develop structures. The case of Alexander the Great is probably the clearest. The case

of Rome is an example of the opposite; there may have been good leaders, consuls and emperors, but there was also a good structure (the Senate, Law, communications, measurements, etc.) capable of providing the system with stability.

Chapter 4

1 The solid black and white lines represent the increase in complexity occurring in the FBK Database as a whole over time. Complexity can be seen to increase notably over time. The dashed lines represent the increase in family complexity (white) and business complexity (black) occurring within the various models identified. They represent the increase in complexity that would occur if the family businesses did not change model. The fact that the increase in complexity occurring in the sample of family businesses as a whole is greater than that occurring in the models indicates that the family businesses change model with the passing of time. If this change of model did not happen, the increase in complexity reflected in the reality of the FBK Database could not occur.

2 Mintzberg has given a brilliant account of this subject (H. Mintzberg, *The Rise and Fall of Strategic Planning*, Prentice Hall, 1994).

3 A balancing loop is an effect generated parallel to any positive development. Thus, for example, an increase in the competitiveness of a firm will cause a rise in wages, which in turn will have a negative effect on competitiveness (P. M. Senge, *The Fifth Discipline: The Art and Practice of the Learning Organization*, Currency Doubleday, New York, 1990).

4 The sign indicates whether the effect of one variable on another is positive or negative.

5 Symmetrically.

6 Jaume Filella distinguishes three types of leadership: effective, social and mental, depending on whether they focus on solving problems, uniting people or glimpsing the future. J. Filella, *Influencia, poder y liderazgo* (Influence, power and leadership), ESADE, working paper, 2001.

7 See the section 'Differences Management' in the annex (p. 156).

8 This process is based on the procedural logic developed by Herbert Simon (H. A. Simon, *Reason in Human Affairs*, Basil Blackwell, 1983).

9 Symmetrically.

10 The FIG can also coexist with other models as well as the Emperor Model.

11 This procedure was proposed by Van der Hayden et al. (L. Van der Hayden, C. Blondel and R. Carlock, 'Fair process: striving for justice in family business', Family Business Review, vol. 18, No. 1, pp. 1–21, San Francisco, 2005) and defined as fair process. It consists in following

a process that provides all those involved with a recognized and legitimate voice, ensures clarity and information sharing between all the participants, applies homogeneous criteria regardless of the person or subject concerned, and allows for the review of decisions as required by the appearance of new information or circumstances.

12 R. Fischer and W. Ury, *Getting to Yes: Negotiating Agreement Without Giving In*, Penguin, New York, 1991.

13 FBK Database, 2007.

14 Term used in industrial economics to refer to investments made for a specific purpose that become useless if the purpose changes. In this case we refer to vital investments made in training or in renouncing alternative careers in order to run the family business in the future.

15 Tagiuri and Davis (1996) performed an excellent study, cited above (footnote 10, Chapter 1 this volume), on labour relations between parents and their children, depending on the moment in the life cycle in which the former and the latter find themselves.

16 J. Filella, 2001, op. cit. (footnote 7, this chapter).

17 Page 52, expanded on p. 156.

18 By reference families we mean the family of origin of the in-laws.

19 The Swedish Wallenberg family set up as a FIG in 1916. Their company (Investor AB, www.investorab.com) is currently estimated to control approximately 30% of the Swedish stock market.

20 Andrew Carnegie was the founder of the Carnegie Steel Company (subsequently US Steel).

21 The creator of the family fortune was Mark Hanna (1837–1904), an entrepreneur in the shipping, coal and steel industry.

22 The Pitcairns have been developing their family office with great success for approximately 90 years. Its success has brought them to open this service up to third parties, by offering multifamily office services (www.pitcairn.com).

23 Corporación Alba is the March family's FIG. It is listed on the stock exchange and holds shares both in firms with widely dispersed shareholdings (ACS, Acerinox) and in other family businesses (Prosegur, Ros Roca).

24 Family/business differentiation, management practices, communication and succession.

25 The term 'private equity' refers to the activity of taking over listed or non-listed companies whose managers or owners are unable to make the most of their companies' potential. The aim is usually to resell the company four or five years later with a large capital gain. This is obtained through improving the management of the business, together with the high indebtedness with which these operations are conducted. These companies arose in the 1980s with specialized firms that managed large funds. More recently, family offices have taken up this practice.

Annex

1 Along these lines, a well-known Belgian family has created the Family Academy, a training programme for all the members of the next generation (300 people) and the present one (50).

2 This is not to say that the prestige of all its members diminishes; rather, the prestige derived from belonging to that family. Obviously, there may be individual members who retain great social prestige.

3 There are significant differences in the functioning of the board depending on its composition. The more open it is, the more functional ($\alpha = 0.001$ and $F = 7.073$).

4 D. C. Hambrick and S. Finkelstein, 'Managerial discretion: A bridge between polar views on organizations', in: L. L. Cummings and B. M. Straw (eds), *Research in Organizational Behavior*, JAI Press, Greenwich, vol. 9 (1987), pp. 369–406.

5 R. Birgit, *Four Essays in Corporate Governance*, Proquest Doctoral Dissertations, University of Chicago, 2002.

6 The Resource-Based View is a strategic approach that holds that companies are distinguishable from each other on the strength of their resource and capability base (assets, individuals, relationships, management systems, coordination systems, level of commitment, technologies, etc.). As a result there are no two companies alike, and this enables them to develop strategies in order to take full advantage of their resources. For example, Honda makes good internal combustion engines, so it develops products based on good engines (cars, motorcycles, outboard motors, lawnmowers, chainsaws, electric generators, etc.).

7 By competence we mean the ability to achieve goals that have been set (R. G. McGrath, I. MacMillan and S. Venkataraman, 'Defining and developing competence: a strategic process paradigm', *Strategic Management Journal*, vol. 1, 1995, pp. 251–275). In this case the goals are set by the Family Council.

8 In the FBK Database, 48% of Spanish management committees studied were found to be unacquainted with their firm's operating account, despite the fact that this information is available in the business register and can be accessed online by means of several databases.

9 M. C. Jensen and W. H. Meckling, 'Theory of the firm: managerial behaviour, agency costs and ownership structure', *Journal of Financial Economics*, No. 3 (1976), pp. 305–360.

10 This means that two or more individuals with the same rank in the family hierarchy (e.g., same generation) also have the same rank in the company hierarchy. In this way, certain hierarchical levels may be reserved for certain generations, giving rise to situations in which, for example, 'top management is for the seniors'.

11 An assessment center is an evaluation methodology in which a group of people, or sometimes a single individual, undergo tests and simulations

designed to facilitate the observation and assessment of their skill profile.

12 The correlation between these two dimensions is significant (r = 0.237).

13 There are some very interesting examples of formally very exigent family constitutions drawn up by families with very low Family accountability. In these cases, executives are perfectly aware that the family constitution is just an aesthetic exercise.

14 In those cases when a Board of Directors exists.

15 G. Squires, 'Management as a professional discipline', *Journal of Management Studies*, vol. 38, No. 4 (2001), pp. 473–488.

16 See footnote 3, Chapter 4.

17 I. Nonaka and H. Takeuchi, *The Knowledge-Creating Company*, Oxford University Press, Oxford, 1995.

18 The correlation between these two dimensions is very high (c = 0.884). FBK Database, 2007.

19 'Up-down' relationships are characterized by complementarity and 'across' relationships by symmetry (P. Watzlawick, J. Beavin and D. Jackson, *Pragmatics of Human Communication: A Study of Interactional Patterns, Pathologies, and Paradoxes*, W. W. Norton & Company, 1967).

20 Stopford and Baden-Fuller, 1994.

21 Technically this is known as the 'fuzzy' approach. This term was coined by Lotfi Zadeh (1965), precursor of the study of fuzzy logic.

22 R. M. Grant, 'The resource-based theory of competitive advantage: implications for strategy formulation', *California Management Review*, vol. 33, No. 3 (1991), pp. 114–136.

23 Here we define the dimension as 'non-dependence on the top executive' so that a high development of this dimension will have a positive value.

Note: Page numbers in italics indicate figures.